W9-BVS-049

*Walking on the Wings
of the Wind*

Walking on the Wings of the Wind

Archbishop Rembert G. Weakland, O.S.B.

PAULIST PRESS
New York/Ramsey

Copyright © 1980 by
Rembert G. Weakland

All rights reserved. No part of this book may be reproduced or transmit-
ted in any form or by any means, electronic or mechanical, including
photocopying, recording or by any information storage and retrieval
system, without permission in writing from the publisher.

Library of Congress
Catalog Card Number: 80-82088

ISBN: 0-8091-2334-7

Published by Paulist Press
Editorial Office: 1865 Broadway, New York, N.Y. 10023
Business Office: 545 Island Road, Ramsey, N.J. 07446

Printed and bound in the United States of America.

Contents

Preface

St. Jerome began his homilies on that source and teacher of all prayer, the Psalter, by calling it a stately mansion. Within it he saw many separate chambers. Only one key, however, could be found to it, namely, the Holy Spirit. Under the guidance of the Spirit one could meditate on God's word with perseverance, so that eventually one did not fear the law but took delight in it.

Next, St. Jerome faced up to that old dilemma of how to pray day and night, without ceasing (1 Thess. 5:17). He described the intimate relationship between prayer and action in this way: "Even if I merely stretch forth my hand in almsgiving, I am meditating on the law of God; if I do what is prescribed, I am praying with my whole body what others are praying with their lips." Prayer and action are seen here as two aspects of the same spiritual attitude.

Perhaps the most insidious deterrent to a persistent search to make prayer a part of our daily existence—like breathing—is the tendency to grow weary. The temptation to rely on ourselves and on our own strength can prevent us from arriving at true prayer. To pray constantly we must have a strong conviction that the power of God in the abiding presence of His Holy Spirit overcomes our weakness, our tiredness. His Spirit is all powerful and teaches us how to pray.

His Spirit is depicted so often in Scripture as fire or as wind, manifestations of that overwhelming divine presence. Through God's goodness, kindness, and mercy toward us that Spirit becomes ours; with God we too, then, can "walk on the wings of the wind" (Psalm 104).

The meditations published in this book appeared originally in *The Catholic Herald Citizen*, diocesan newspaper of the Archdiocese of Milwaukee. They are really about prayer, not in a narrow sense, but as it affects the whole of life. At times they talk about how to pray, at times they are prayers, at times they lead to change of attitude or to action. Ultimately, they all spring from meditation on God's word. They are meant, not for the savants, but for the little people, the simple of heart.

I would like to thank the faithful of the Archdiocese of Milwaukee—clerical and lay alike—who encouraged me to share these insights. I must also express my gratitude to the many hidden contributors who supplied an idea or an image and where I could never trace back the source, long forgotten.

Teach Us to Pray

Prayer and Life

At times praying can be difficult for us: we feel empty and find it impossible to untangle our confused, inmost feelings. At other times we find it easy to pour out our hearts to God, who seems so personal and so near. All of this, however, should not surprise us nor startle us. Praying is related to life; it is a way of life. Prayer is very much related to the events of each day and our responses to them.

Christ himself should be our example of a person of prayer. How differently he prays at times! After his disciples had returned and, full of excitement, had related to him the stories of their first ministry, filled with the joy of the Holy Spirit, he prayed: "I bless you, Father, Lord of heaven and earth, for hiding these things from the learned and clever and revealing them to mere children" (Lk. 10:21). But later, reflecting on the death that was to come, he exclaimed: "Now my soul is troubled. What shall I say: Father, save me from this hour? But it was for this very reason that I came to this hour" (Jn. 12:27-28). One prayer springs from joy, the other from anguish.

It is in the gospel of St. Luke in particular where we see Christ as a person of prayer and where we discover that

Christ's prayer is always intimately related to the important events and moments in his life and has a close relationship also to his search to conform to his Father's will. His prayer, too, is under the impulse of the Spirit. Let us look at some of the moments in Christ's life when Luke tells us Christ was at prayer.

All of these elements are present at the moment he was baptized by John. "While Jesus after his own baptism was at prayer, heaven opened and the Holy Spirit descended on him in bodily shape, like a dove" (Lk. 3:21-22).

The choice of the twelve men who were to constitute his most intimate followers was an important event. "Now it was about this time that he went out into the hills to pray; and he spent the whole night in prayer to God. When day came, he summoned his disciples and picked out twelve of them; he called them 'apostles' " (Lk. 6:12-14).

After the miracle of the loaves and fishes we can say that Jesus' popularity had reached its height. John tells us the people were about to come and take him by force and make him king (Jn. 6:15). Matthew tells us that he escaped from the crowd and went up into the hills by himself to pray (Matt. 14:23). In the gospel of Luke this moment of prayer after the great miracle of the multiplication of the loaves and fishes is succeeded by Peter's famous profession of faith. "Now when he was praying alone in the presence of his disciples . . . he said: 'But you, who do you say I am?' It was Peter who spoke up. 'The Christ of God,' he said" (Lk. 9:18-21).

One of the most important moments in Jesus' life, as he revealed himself to his most intimate disciples, was the Transfiguration. "He took with him Peter and John and James and went up to the mountain to pray. As he prayed, the aspect of his face was changed and his clothing became brilliant as lightning" (Lk. 9:28-29).

The prayer he taught his disciples was the result of his own prayer. "Now once he was in a certain place praying, and when he had finished, one of his disciples said, 'Lord, teach us to pray. . . .'" He said to them, "Say this when you pray: Father, may your name be held holy" (Lk. 11:1-2).

In the light of this background of a life where every important moment occurred with the accompaniment of prayer there is no surprise when, faced with immediate death, he went to the Mount of Olives. "He withdrew from his disciples, about a stone's throw away, and knelt down and prayed. 'Father,' he said, 'if you are willing, take this cup away from me. Nevertheless, let your will be done, not mine'" (Lk. 22:39-42).

Before important moments in his life and mission we find Jesus spending whole nights in prayer. We see that these moments of prayer were closely linked with his search to do the will of his Father—not to take the easy and popular way out. Although Christ was both human and divine, it should not scandalize us that he struggled—and we see this in his prayer— to ascertain and conform to the will of his Father, not his own will.

All of us face that complicated problem of doing what God wants; we, too, search so often in our lives for God's will. There is no clear, unequivocal formula for finding that will, but one thing is certain: only in prayer, when we are alone with God, will our own selfishness be revealed and will we have that peace and serenity that are necessary for seeing what he wants of us. Finding God's will in our lives is always a struggle, but we struggle in vain to find it if we have not developed a lifestyle that reverts constantly to moments of being alone with God.

There should, thus, be no dichotomy between our daily lives and our moments of prayer. As in the example of Jesus, the events of life spontaneously lead to prayer: moments of thanks and joy, or periods of anguish and searching. There should be a constant rhythmic flow in our lives from prayer to event and back to prayer. Slowly we begin then to understand how the presence of the same Spirit in both event and prayer creates a unity in our lives and a sense of the ever-abiding presence of God in us and around us.

3

For this reason I said that praying is a way of life, not just isolated, unrelated moments of existence.

Praise and thanksgiving

Prayer is not just a few moments that we take each day to be alone with God. It really springs from a lifestyle and a whole attitude toward life that is based on a deep and profound faith. For this reason I would like to write about one of those attitudes which is fundamental for any prayer, namely, *awe* or *wonder*.

In reading the accounts of the birth of Christ in St. Matthew's and St. Luke's gospels, we find that this attitude of awe and mystery leaps from every line. Zachary and Elizabeth, Joseph and Mary, Simeon and Anna—each one exemplifies fully such an attitude of marvel and wonder. As they stand before God's loving way of dealing with them, in the mystery that surrounds and shrouds his ways, they project their awe and reverence in prayer.

Have you ever visited the Grand Canyon or Kilimanjaro? Have you ever stood on the bank and watched the ocean roar? Have you ever flown high above the clouds and looked down at the smallness of the earth and its creatures? Before all these manifestations of nature we stand in awe. How well I remember the trip a few years back across the Sinai Desert in the hot sun when suddenly I saw the little Monastery of St. Catherine at the base of that gigantic mountain of rock. As I looked up at that natural fortress, I said to myself that truly God could speak from here.

And then there is a Bach fugue, a Mozart symphony, or Dave Brubeck at the piano, or a Rembrandt, or a Michelangelo, or a Frank Lloyd Wright. Do you remember the first time you saw an amoeba under a microscope, or traced a comet?

Hopefully, you have met older people who still retain that

4

sense of discovery, who are always amazed at something new, who are always being astonished—just like perpetual novices. They never permit themselves to grow cynical, to become closed-minded, to lose their curiosity and their sense of grandeur, mystery, and majesty.

This attitude of awe and wonderment by itself, however, is not prayer, but it is basic to any prayer. It can lead one to make those utterances that one finds so often in the Gospel of glorifying and thanking God. For a Christian such utterances of prayer must become a habit.

Full of wonder and awe at the way in which God was dealing with her, Mary broke forth into that perfect hymn of praise, "My soul glorifies the Lord, and my spirit exults in God my Savior" (Lk. 1:47-55). Zachary, filled with marvel at the events surrounding the birth of John the Baptist, raised his voice in praise to God, "Blessed be the Lord, the God of Israel, for he has visited his people" (Lk. 1:68-79). At Bethlehem at the crib there appeared a multitude of angels praising God and saying, "Glory to God in the highest" (Lk. 2:14). Christ himself taught us to pray, saying, "When you pray, say: 'Father, hallowed be thy Name'" (Lk. 11:2). After raising Lazarus from the dead, he exclaimed, "Father, I thank you that you have heard me" (Jn. 11:41). These examples show how that attitude of wonder and awe led spontaneously to prayers of glorifying and thanking God.

For a moment now think of some of your friends and thank God for them. Think of your parents, relatives, and loved ones and thank God for them. Think of those in need who rely on you for help, comfort, and aid, and permit you to be more Christ-like and thank God for them.

Remember the beautiful sunsets that you have gazed on and glorify God. Remember the beauty of the faces of children and old people whom you have seen and glorify God. Remember the beautiful music you have heard and glorify God.

Just gaze one moment on the mystery of your own human

body and thank and glorify God.

Keep alive to his wonders that surround you and try daily to marvel at the people and objects that come your way and glorify God. See his hand in every event and thank him.

Especially in times of suffering, as you share his cross and gaze on the symbols of the nails and thorns in your own life, praise and thank him for the possibility of sharing more deeply in the mystery of his cross and resurrection and glorify God.

The little people's breviary

Have you ever watched a priest recite his Office? Perhaps you saw him use all five fingers as markers to keep the place straight, while he murmured words with his lips. There was always something mysterious about that gilt-edged, black leather book and its contents. (At least it used to be black!)

In order to understand the Divine Office, three points should be kept in mind.

First of all, the Breviary is meant to be a complement to the Mass and extend its thrust throughout the entire day. We must imagine Christ as Eternal High Priest, but attaching to himself the entire human community, continuously offering to the Father his song of praise and interceding for the salvation of the whole world. This scene is "imaged" in each diocese as the clergy and faithful unite with their bishop—if not bodily, at least in intention—in offering praise to the Father and petitioning for the needs of the church through Jesus. Bishops and priests are seen primarily as people of continuous prayer in union with Jesus.

Secondly, since to pray incessantly is physically impossible, moments of prayer were introduced to coincide with the changing time cycle of each day, morning and evening prayer becoming the pivotal points. A noonday prayer is also an integral part of the new Breviary. (The older devotion included a prayer break—note, not a coffee break—also at 9 a.m. and 3 p.m. The night vigil of prayer was characteristic of the monks.)

Thirdly, the Divine Office also took advantage of the time cycle of the week and the year, in order to celebrate the mysteries of the life and death of Jesus. The cycle of nature became the hinges around which the major events in the life of our Lord pivoted. Easter, with its preparatory period of Lent, and Christmas, with its preparatory period of Advent, were central.

Thus, the Divine Office pressed the important moments of our Lord's life into yearly celebrations that complement the Mass. It is different from the Mass, however, in having a relationship also to the cycle of each day—sunrise, sunset—night, daytime. One stopped working, if only for a short period of time, in order to focus on Jesus and be in his presence at the throne of the Father as the day began, in the middle of work, and as the day closed.

*   *   *

Two very popular forms of prayer developed as a kind of lay person's breviary: the Angelus and the Rosary. Both of these are Marian devotions in keeping with the medieval concept of the Office where the presence of Mary was always accentuated and often explicitly recalled at the end of each hour.

The Angelus is based on the principle of praying at specific moments of the day—morning, noon, night. It remembers secondarily the mysteries of Jesus' life from birth, to grave, to resurrection.

The Rosary, on the other hand, is based on the meditation of the pivotal events in the life of Jesus and his Mother. It keeps a liturgical base—sorrowful mysteries for Friday, glorious for Sunday.

The Rosary is a perfect prayer: it repeats, like the pleadings of a child, the same words over and over; but it also relates to the entire mystery of salvation.

Those who find the Rosary old-fashioned or outmoded

will change their minds when they are sick or tired or unable to concentrate. It keeps our hands, our heads, our lips occupied—but so gently and without tension.

Why have the Angelus and the Rosary survived so many centuries?

Because they present a perfect theology of Marian devotion, in that they are always so closely related to the whole picture of salvation through Jesus.

Prayer of petition

As we grow older, each one of us passes through a period of doubt with regard to our prayers of petition. As children we were so accustomed to ask for things from our parents and elders that it was normal for us to pray in the same way. Without too much sophistication we just repeated "gimme" till we wore the other out.

Then came that period of doubt. "If God knows everything, then why do we have to tell him our needs?" "Surely God's not going to change his plans just because we ask him." "I pray and pray for things, but nothing ever happens." And so on.

But when we read again the gospel of St. Luke, we find that Christ himself prayed frequently to his Father and taught us, too, to pray for our needs and the needs of others. For example, Christ said to Peter, in foretelling Peter's denial of him: "But I have prayed for you, Simon, that your faith may not fail, and once you have recovered, you in your turn must strengthen your brothers" (Lk. 22:32). Who can forget Jesus' cry from the cross: "Father, forgive them; they do not know what they are doing" (Lk. 23:34).

Christ not only showed his disciples by example how to pray, but he explicitly taught his disciples and us some very important aspects of prayer of petition. For example, he told us that God, as a loving Father, listens to our prayer because he

8

loves us. The story of the prodigal son shows exactly how much God loves us. His concern extends to everyone and to every detail of our life—regardless of how insignificant it all seems. The lilies of the field are nothing compared to us (Matt. 6:25-34). Just as the Father listened to Christ, so he will listen to us: "Ask, and it will be given to you; search, and you will find; knock, and the door will be opened to you" (Matt. 7:7-11). Who could be untouched by that most solemn prayer of Jesus to his Father at the Last Supper and recorded by St. John in chapter 17 of his gospel when he prays for his disciples before leaving him.

Seeing how Christ prayed to his Father and how he teaches us to pray for our needs, we must admit that the problem must lie in us and in our concept of God. First of all, we should not think of ourselves as "saying prayers," as if they were forms to be filled out and sent through the mail. We must really talk to God as a friend—as a child to a loving parent. Of course, he knows our difficulty. But could we fail to want to communicate to a friend even when we know that friend understands? Then we must also realize that God doesn't normally act as if he were performing magic tricks to make our life easy so we could pass through it without challenge, without suffering, without doubt, without growing up. God's usual way of answering prayers is by helping things to grow back into line. Growth takes time. If there is a tree outside your window, it probably looks the same size today as it looked yesterday. But it isn't. Do not be surprised if you do not see the answer to your prayers at once. In fact, some of the most important aspects of life, like thinking and loving, work invisibly too. They cannot be measured.

It is easy for us to understand that a parent wants only the best for a child and will respond in the best interests of the child, even if the child does not understand what is at that moment best for him. But we are adults and we have our own reasoning processes to account for. Here we come to the crux of the problem. All our prayers have as an underlying assumption: "Thy will be done." Without this faith all prayer is really empty words. Every prayer we utter reaches the Father, through Christ, and is under the impulse of the Spirit. Even our most private prayer is a part of this larger dimension and is not isolated from the whole history of salvation.

Christ himself said: "If you have faith, everything you ask for in prayer you will receive" (Matt. 21:22). But later, in the Garden of Olives, he showed us how his own more human inclination to want to avoid suffering conflicted with his Father's will and how, in that confrontation, he was able to accept that will. "My Father, if it is possible, let this cup pass me by. Nevertheless, let it be as you, not I, would have it" (Matt. 26:39). Yes, Jesus begged to escape Good Friday, but by being obedient to his Father's will—not his own human weakness—he came to the glory of Easter Sunday.

Do not forget that we need Faith, not only to pray this way, but to see the answers to our prayer. Secondly, never grow tired in praying. Jesus tells us to be persistent. Our Faith grows in that very persistency. Lastly, let us never forget that there will always be a certain mystery involved in prayer, simply because the other partner is God himself. The answers to all our questions about prayer will have to wait till we know him fully.

Till then, let us follow the wisdom Paul wrote to the Thessalonians: "Be happy at all times; *pray constantly*; and for all things give thanks to God, because this is what God expects you to do in Christ Jesus" (1 Thess. 5:18).

The point of silence

The finest aspect of prayer is that it can be at its best when we are at our worst. For almost everything else we do in life we have to be in shape.

Prayer is also at its best when we have nowhere else to turn. God doesn't mind. He is there waiting. We smile about no atheists in the foxholes, but the best moments for prayer are when we find ourselves helpless.

Wanting to be self-sufficient is natural for the human person. It is a question of our own pride and dignity. Even when all seems to be going wrong, there is reluctance to give in; we keep up a good front and hide our condition from others. But God is always there—waiting.

How often we find this mood expressed by the psalmist! Everyone—everything—has proven false; only the support of Yahweh remains constant, unfaltering, secure. Time and time again we have had to relearn that lesson; it has to be learned in the life of a people, a nation, in the life of each individual. At one point or another we learn that everything can be taken from us and the whole of life can change course, but one aspect remains unchanged—our faith in God's love.

We all learn of this love in different ways and at different periods of life—some early, some later—but it eventually becomes a reality to us. God is happy and rejoices when we learn it. He never says, "I told you so."

The opposite moment is also a true one. At times we are so full of joy that we cry out for someone with whom we can share that joy. No one seems quite able to understand our feelings; we cannot express ourselves adequately nor convey the full power of our emotion.

But God is there!

How often, too, the psalmist experienced that feeling of praising God for all the good things that happened. Just one "alleluia" suffices.

Or perhaps we have just read a poem, or heard a piece of music, or seen a bird in flight, and there is no way of expressing our wonderment and awe, of articulating and sharing the insight. But, like the psalmist, we find that God is there.

Can another person ever truly understand exactly how we feel? I claim that there is one point of our being where we are alone, that is incommunicable to any other—whether we be celibate or married, have deep friendships or but passing

11

acquaintances. We can share that moment only with God, because no explanation is necessary. Prayer means turning toward him, because we know he understands.

At the deepest moments of prayer, words, thus, become unnecessary, useless, even an impediment, whether the moment to be shared is one of anguish or extreme joy.

"O Lord, you search me and you know me,
you know my resting and my rising,
you discern my purpose from afar.
You mark when I walk or lie down,
all my ways lie open to you.
Before even a word is on my tongue
you know it, Lord, through and through. . .

"O search me, God, and know my heart.
O test me and know my thoughts.
See that I follow not the wrong path
and lead me in the path of life eternal."

(Psalm 138)

To all I say, in moments of anguish, in moments of joy, when alone, when with others—"The Lord be with you!"

Advent and Christmas

Emmanuel—God among us

"Come, Lord Jesus, come!"

How often during the Advent season I have said these words, dear Jesus. Teach me to understand what they really mean.

Come to me, Jesus, in my weakness, in my sinfulness.

That coming, I know, will be more like iodine on an open sore. My faults are so exposed, like open wounds; but after the burning sensation comes the healing lotions that soothe and mend.

Come to me, Jesus, in my moments of doubt and insecurity.

How difficult it is to be a bishop! So many demands and expectancies from these clay feet. Lord, I have my moments of self-doubt, too. Why must people think it is I who must have a solution to everything? Or are they only looking for an ear that will listen to their hurts?

Come to me, Jesus, in my moments of depression and discouragement.

I try, really, Lord, to teach your gospel and put it into practice; but my words are so often twisted against me— sometimes even by friends, almost as if they were eager to see

13

me tripped up. Teach me to see, Jesus, that you are able to bring good out of wrong and order out of confusion; teach me to see and understand the hurts in others that lie beneath the twists.

Come to me, Jesus, in my moments of tiredness and irritability.

Give me always, Jesus, the strength to go out to one more hurting person, one more soul in need, one more group to be touched.

Come to me, Jesus, in my moments of arrogance and pride. (It is not easy, Jesus, to say that and mean it.)

Yes, I do need to be brought down so very often. Too much adulation, too much praise is not good for a bishop. One moment of silence, though, and I see the facade crumble. Come to me in those moments, pick me up, sustain me.

Come to me, Jesus, in my moments of joy.

When I am at the altar or with good friends, or at the piano, or just walking along the streets greeting people, come to me through all these moments of pleasure and teach me to rejoice in you.

Come, Jesus, come!

What an empty life it would be, Jesus, if you did not come at Christmas and bring together into one solemn encounter all those moments of weakness and strength, depression and solace, sorrow and joy!

Come, Lord Jesus, come!

Waiting

One of my clearest recollections as a boy during the war years involved my cousin, Mary, whose husband, Jack, was fighting in the Pacific. Each night we watched her write long, long letters, page after page, although we knew that nothing really happened in our hometown. And then there were the times we would catch her staring at his high school photo on

14

the mantel, where he looked so silly with that shiny, sleek black hair.

But, finally the word came that the war was coming to an end and he was expected home. Then even stranger things happened. Mary went on a diet; she went to the hairdresser's; she painted the living room; she sent all the kids to the dentist; she cooked all his old favorite dishes to make sure they hadn't been forgotten. The letters became longer, even though there seemed little chance he would ever get them.

We were all waiting, but Mary's waiting was special. Hers is what you could have called a "creative expectancy," waiting for one who is loved and also preparing for his coming.

In a sense Advent elicits these same emotions. We live in expectancy of the coming of Christ on three levels. Through the liturgical text of the Old Testament we live with the Jews of old in a world that is waiting for a Savior, a Redeemer, a Messiah. We dream of the changed world that will come about through his being with us..Then we relive the coming of Christ into history and into our own personal history. He came, he changed, he transformed us. But we also cast our glance toward his coming again in fullness to make that transformation of us and this world complete.

But these waitings are not like sitting in a doctor's office till it's our turn. Instead, we are creating, preparing, making ourselves and this world around us more Christ-like. Thus, a Christian waits in this world by involvement.

But here my image falls short. Our creative involvement in this world is not just our own doing. Christ, having once come into our history on the first Christmas, continues to be "involved." It is he who continues to create. Our task must be an involvement with him and his plan. Sometimes our logic does not follow his, but we seek to be worthy instruments for the changing, the redeeming, the transforming of this world. Theologians call this process "Incarnationalism," that is, the way in which the power of that first Incarnation continues to work to the end of time.

15

Why is this important? On the one hand, we Christians must avoid a kind of "spiritualistic" attitude toward the problems of this world around us that would seek salvation by jumping over the world instead of going through it. Secondly, we must avoid that temptation of equating worldly logic with Christ's design and his kingdom. A Catholic becomes involved, but in order to make this world a better vehicle for Christ's living presence.

One last thought. We all like the chance to start over again, especially when we have made a mess of things so many times. Advent gives us just such a chance. Each year the church starts her cycle of reflections, presentation, and reliving the Christian mysteries over again with Advent. She wants us to do the same. We have the chance again of letting Christ enter our lives and of becoming involved so that his presence will be felt around us.

Christ the light

"Hear the herald voice resounding:
'Christ is near,' it seems to say,
'Cast away the dreams of darkness,
Welcome Christ, the light of day!' "

The sixth century author of this poem in using the expression, "the herald voice," wished to point to John the Baptist. His task or role in God's plan consisted in announcing that Christ, the Anointed, had come.

The image of light used by the poet to describe Christ and his coming was an old one that found its complete expression in the gospel of St. John. There Christ is compared to the light that comes into this world to dispel the darkness that comes through sin.

Some few years ago I celebrated Mass in India using the new experimental Indian Rite. At the beginning of Mass, in a ceremony similar to our own sprinkling of the congregation with water to remind us of baptism, all present, one by one, placed their hands over the flame of the paschal candle and then brought their hands to the eyes and foreheads.

This symbolic gesture indicated their recognition of the need for Christ as light in order to see and understand his word. It also signified to them the need to be purified as by fire and the need to be full of the flame of the Spirit. All of this is a gesture to say that faith in the Resurrected Christ brings a new vision. It opens our eyes. We see things in a new light.

It was Christ who brought that new vision into our world and into our personal lives. His Resurrection, signified in that paschal candle, is the source of our new life.

All this is true, but it is important not to limit our understanding of Christ and his coming to a purely intellectual knowledge of what God and religion are all about. Christ did not come as a Buddha or a Confucius. Christianity is not just a system containing an intellectual analysis of God, the human race, this world and how they are related. Nor is it just a set of norms of right conduct. It is basically all of these things only because it is a relationship to a person, to Christ himself. He is the vine, we are the branches. He is the Way, the Truth, and the Life. He is the revelation of the Father. He sent his Spirit to teach us all things.

Christianity has never been afraid of all the intellectual and scientific development we human beings can accumulate. On the contrary, and in spite of historical conflicts that have arisen and continue to arise, Christianity is never anti-intellectual, anti-artistic, anti-scientific. But Christ does not equate all of this progress with God's kingdom.

Christianity has always known that people have a heart and emotions. Christ, as a light, penetrates the whole of each human being, one's intellectual strivings to understand, and one's emotional response from the heart in love. St. John in the gospel was also clear in declaring that Christ came into our lives in love. God first loved us and for this reason sent his Son to redeem us. Christianity is, thus, very personal. The same poet wrote:

> "Lord, remember that in love
> Thou didst leave Thy throne above,
> Man's frail nature to assume
> In the holy Virgin's womb."

Have you ever wondered why Christ came as a baby? The gospel says little about Christ growing up, but it does present that appealing image of Christ as a baby. We do not argue and dispute with a baby; we just want to pick him up and draw him close to us. The baby is so defenseless and helpless, but so lovable and accessible. Young-old, rich-poor, all can relate equally to a baby.

During the Christmas season we have in the past emphasized too much this aspect and neglected to see that it is only an aid, a prelude to an important step that must follow. The gospel shows that Christ as a babe was accessible to shepherds and kings, but they immediately saw that he was the Son of God. Only in making that Act of Faith can he become our light in a sinful and dark world.

And so, approach the crib at Christmas with those visible feelings of joy and love; but go beyond them to make an Act of Faith in his divinity, so that you can approach him in the Eucharist, in your neighbor, in those moments of joy and sorrow that will succeed each other in your life. Most of all, remember that Christianity is that relationship between yourself and him. That relationship, even after that Act of Faith, must become personal to you through prayer.

During the Christmas season may his presence fill your heart with joy, peace, and sentiments of love, and your mind with clarity of vision for the future. May the hope he brought be yours.

Violence or peace: a personal choice

Throughout the Christmas season we speak often of peace and love and goodwill among people. But it is so elusive and remains a distant and unattainable utopia.

The world seems still so full of violence. Whatever newspaper we pick up, in whatever part of the world, is full of accounts of acts of violence, often committed without much premeditation, but certainly the result of bitterness and contempt of society—sentiments which, without doubt, have been tormenting people's souls for much time.

Why have we become so insensitive to our neighbors? How can people commit such cruel and terrifying acts without signs of remorse?

I am no psychologist, but I believe that in each one of us there is a bit of that cold cruelty. How often we, too, treat other people as material objects, not as persons! If that *other* is aggressive and selfish, perhaps it is because he or she has never experienced a true and unselfish love on the part of another.

I know that we feel helpless in the face of all that violence. What can we do in a positive way? The problem seems too enormous for our single efforts, true; but to reason thus can also be too easy an escape from our Christian commitment.

If all Christians would imitate the example of Christ and take seriously his Sermon on the Mount, the world would indeed be changed! Mahatma Gandhi understood this aspect of Jesus' message better than most Christians. For him too, *Ahimsa*, or nonviolence, was more than mere passive resistance. It arises out of two Christian values: a sense of the dignity of each individual and the need to arrive at love of God through love of neighbor.

The Christian message of peace is this: If God so loved us that he sent his Son to be one of us, then we do have a great value in his eyes. We, too, then, must value others in the same way. Secondly, we, too, must learn how to love in the same way, caring not for self, but for the other.

For this reason Jesus preached service to others to balance our tendencies toward violence, frustration, jealousy, and envy. This service is not just a form of philanthropy, but an expression of true Christian values. It must become the lifestyle of each Christian.

But perhaps you are saying within you—this is still utopia. Original sin still exists and the world will not change.

Jesus did not think that way. He not only taught disinterested love, but he also gave to us, and continues to give us, the grace needed to conquer within ourselves the old selfish ways.

Thus, the Christian message is one of hope against all odds. It is easy to speak of hope when all goes well; but Christian hope is based on the belief that God cares even when all seems lost and every human force seems inadequate.

We can give others glimpses of such hope by our own example of loving service. Each time we imitate Jesus by a disinterested, loving care of others, we help them overcome the violence within them.

Peace will not come about in one day—but why not strive and work toward this ideal in our own lives each day?

God's Word Transforms Me

Compassion

One of the most touching miracles performed by Christ was the raising from the dead of the son of the widow of Naim (Lk. 7:11-17).

What made this miracle unusual and so different from the rest was the fact that no one pleaded with Jesus to perform it. In the other instances the person, sick or lame, or relatives, or the superior (centurion) begged Jesus to cure or heal the infirmity.

But in this case Jesus is "moved by compassion," by pity, and takes the initiative. Since all the miracles have a symbolic meaning—a manifestation of God's power to heal all of us of our sin—those that involve raising someone from the dead have an even greater depth of imagery to be plumbed.

The compassion or pity that Jesus showed is the same that the Father has for us and is the supreme motive for his sending his Son to us as Savior and then raising him from the dead.

To return, however, to our story: Jesus was moved by compassion. *Compassion* means to suffer with—*cum patire*. Jesus enters fully into the suffering heart of the widow. He is able to understand and make his own her grief. He enters completely into our own lives in the same way. By these signs of pity he shows his full humanness.

21

A second point is worthy of notice. The miracle he performs caused all to be filled with awe and to praise God. They knew that a great prophet had arisen and remembered the stories of similar miracles by the prophets, Elijah and Elisha.

The event was to them a sign that God visited his people. God's presence was made known again.

Our task is to imitate Jesus in his compassion. To be Christ-like means to be moved by other people's sorrow, to enter fully into their suffering situation, to be sensitive to their grief and pain.

To be moved by compassion is more than a superficial or intellectual analysis. The heart is touched to do something— regardless of how small it is—to show identity with the one suffering and to be of help.

By these gestures on our part, we, too, make visible to others the presence of the saving power of God. We see the kindness of others as signs of God's care and concern for us. God's presence is made known through gestures of love and kindness.

Then we, too, can be full of awe and praise of God, saying, "Blessed be the Lord, the God of Israel, for he has visited his people, he has come to their rescue" (Lk. 1:68).

Loving and being lovable

Several years ago a venerable old Buddhist monk told me he disliked very much the Catholic concept of love. My reaction was astonishment, because the concept of love found in the New Testament, and especially in the writings of St. John, seemed to me to be one of the most beautiful aspects of the whole Gospel message. I waited curiously for his explanation.

"Christian love," he said, "is too aggressive; it wants to embrace everybody—whether the others like it or not. It is too possessive. Wouldn't it be better," he continued, "if people only tried to be more lovable, to present themselves before others as lovable people?"

There is a grain of truth in what the old Buddhist was saying. We could, and should, be more lovable creatures. If we would only make ourselves easy to love! It is truly Christian to develop those virtues that make us lovable—tenderness, affability, long-suffering, understanding, respectfulness, patience, and the like.

Perhaps one of the reasons why the old Buddhist felt this way comes from our own false notion and projection of Christian love. True Christian love is not possessive and it is not aggressive. It is always an imitation—an extension—of God's love for us. Its greatest expression is that imitation of Christ's own love which impelled him to lay down his life for us. "A man can have no greater love than to lay down his life for his friends" (Jn. 15:13).

Love seeks not its own good, but the good of the other. It does not try to change people so they become like oneself, but respects them and lets them be what they are. In fact, if we truly wish to imitate Christ, then we must learn to love people precisely because they are poor, sinful, weak, and in need. That is how Christ loves us.

You remember certainly, St Paul's description of Christian love in the letter to the Corinthians: "Love is always patient and kind; it is never jealous; love is never boastful or conceited; it is never rude or selfish; it does not take offense, and is not resentful. Love takes no pleasure in other people's sins but delights in truth; it is always ready to excuse, to trust, to hope, and to endure whatever comes" (1 Cor. 13:4-7). If our love has these qualities, we will also be lovable.

Among the aspects of love that St. Paul mentions let me single out this phrase: it is ready to trust and to hope and to endure whatever comes. These qualities are especially important in our day. We have all grown too cynical to love fully in a Christian way. Trusting others is basic for love. God had every

23

reason to abandon his unfaithful people; he would have every reason to abandon each one of us. Yet the beautiful lesson to be learned from the Old Testament is that God remains faithful even when man does not return his love. And he so loved the world that he sent his only Son as our Savior. It is this love we must imitate. It is easy to love those who have given signs of meriting our trust; it is Christian to love those who do not.

And love is ready to endure whatever comes. How necessary this quality of endurance is today! We speak much of the need for permanency in marriage, but that kind of permanency will come only if the love that sustains it is willing to endure whatever comes. St. Paul knew well that love grows and matures through suffering and endurance. It grows only with time. We need that kind of fidelity in love if marriage is to become stable. But each one of us in all our relationships with others must be willing to endure whatever comes if we want to grow in friendship and the love that is basic to it. Growth in love comes through such challenges.

Perhaps it is precisely in those moments when we seem lacking in signs of trust and must endure the sufferings that come with love that we must try to be lovable. Being lovable is the other side of the coin of loving.

Simplicity

There is a whole segment of the Gospel that we find difficult to accept, or at least to put into practice. I refer to those texts that describe our inner attitude in relationship to the world.

Jesus tells us to be like sheep or doves—mild, gentle, simple. Christians get no prize for diplomacy, but only for sincerity and authenticity. Before the complexity of this world Jesus advises an inner simplicity and detachment.

The world is indeed complicated and its problems require complex solutions, but the Christian does not permit that world to keep his or her life from having a clear direction. Our lives must be brought into focus in spite of that complicated world, and, in a very special sense, in order to help that world.

Christian simplicity relates to the ordinary tasks of everyday existence. Doing the ordinary well, bringing to it a sense of love and hope, keeping that inner peace and tranquility that comes from Faith in Divine Providence is what simplicity is all about. The little things count. That's where the action is.

Early monastic literature is full of spiritual advice on purity of heart and much of that wisdom survived into the Middle Ages in the training of the knights. All the external, physical, ascetical training needed to face the multi-faceted evil of society was accompanied by an inner docility and clarity that came with self-knowledge and sincerity. Purity of heart meant nobility of intention, clarity of emotion, and the peace that comes from a lack of guile.

The opposite of purity of heart is duplicity, selfishness, unfulfilled ambition, and jealousy.

Simplicity and purity of heart also imply a clear knowledge of our needs and freedom and detachment from unnecessary and encumbering desires. One can have nothing and still be eaten up with senseless longings that lead to frustration and bitterness. Physical poverty does not necessarily lead to detachment and simplicity.

Nor is a Christian a stoic. A Christian is not impassive to joy and pleasure and sorrow. All these emotions are present, but given direction and scope because of a deep Faith in Divine Providence.

The great saints seemed all to have that simplicity of vision. Benedict, St. Gregory tells us, saw the whole world at a glance, as if bathed in a single vision of light. Francis was the finest model of Christian simplicity and clarity in his relationship to this world. By and how to live without excess baggage and needs. We all know the life of the Little Flower, and so many others.

Perhaps the world today is calling out to all of us to save it by taking more seriously the evangelical call to simplicity. Perhaps the energy crisis is a grace-filled moment for all of us, forcing us to examine our lifestyle and bring it back into focus. We can offer no simple solutions to the world's problems, but we can live with an inner peace and wholeness when our lives are centered on the Gospel's simplicity—no unneeded baggage, no falseness.

Live simply—in the Lord.

Humor

We all take ourselves too seriously. Learning to laugh at oneself can be a healing experience. It can only happen, however, when we are sure of who we are and can afford to smile at that amusing reality.

Where does religion enter into all of this? True, religion should give us a sense, first of all, of our own worth. We are important to God because he is concerned about each one of us. On this conviction rests our sense of self-assurance.

Each person has been created into a unique image of God—no two alike, no series. That makes me special. When Jesus mentioned that one should love one's neighbor as oneself he certainly must have thought we should begin with self-esteem and a good self-love.

I am always amazed at how many people do not have this good feeling about their unique self. They must be constantly encouraged and their worth must be affirmed and pointed out over and over again to them. If each one of us could rise each day with full trust and confidence in God's goodness and in his care for us, how much more joy and happiness we would all bring into the world.

If we lack a good self-image, then we tend to compensate by trying to degrade others and make them look bad, we tend to cover up by facades—that everyone sees through. We live then in a false and insecure world.

Sometimes we arrive at this weak self-image through faulty comparisons with others. We see ourselves as clumsy and stupid, others as coordinated and bright. Most of the time we are comparing apples and oranges. We tend to be envious people because of such a false self-image.

Every mistake, every sign of weakness becomes a major crisis, because our mask tends to fall and we have to face ourselves as we are. Failure turns into catastrophe.

But, when we have full confidence in God's sustaining love, we can take delight in human foibles—especially our own. We can smile at our mistakes and learn from them. Humor then becomes a lovable part of being human. We accept being who we are with a certain thankfulness and joy.

The Bible is not full of slapstick humor, but the just man does accept the human condition with compassion and realism. The Bible is not embarrassed by such little things as the droppings that blind Tobit. The Bible never hides deep joy and deep love.

Of course, hell and the devil exist. But a religion that talks about nothing but these cannot be sound. One has to have the confidence to laugh even at the devil. That is what salvation is all about.

Yes, we all take ourselves too seriously—for the wrong reasons. I am sure God looks on us and smiles a lot when he sees our petty concerns.

We all in the church today should pray for more humor.

Rash judgment

Recently an old prayer book fell into my hands. In browsing through it I saw a list of sins to be used for the examination of conscience before confession.

One among the sins attracted my special attention: rash judgment. How long it has been since I heard (or preached) a sermon on that topic!

(We could all benefit from looking again at old lists such as that one. I had the feeling that most of those sins are still around, even though they are not mentioned as often today.)

How frequently Jesus warned against rash judgment!

"If you want to avoid judgment, stop passing judgment. Your verdict on others will be the verdict passed on you. The measure with which you measure will be used to measure you" (Matt. 7:1-2). "Why look at the speck in your brother's eye, when you miss the plank in your own?" (Matt. 7:3-4).

Christ's treatment of the woman caught in adultery showed not harsh judgment—but forgiving compassion.

If modern psychology teaches us anything, it is the difficulty involved in analyzing the ultimate motivation behind actions, not just in others, but in ourselves as well. So many actions are the result of unreflected fears and insecurities that lie deep in our subconscious. The opposite, too, happens. Often our motives are good, but in the execution it all seems to come out topsy-turvy and not at all as planned. We feel miserable because we just didn't measure up.

Needless to say, we have all, too, been victims of rash judgment and probably suffered much because of it. Perhaps people easily attributed motives to our actions on little or no evidence. Most of us become a bit used to it—but never entirely. How often our friendships have been strained forever by such false accusations.

Yet we continue to hurt others with our rash and amateurish psychological analysis of their motives. Nowadays rash judgment has simply become more sophisticated. Everyone has a smattering of psychology and a basic vocabulary of scientific terms, so as to label others in a more plausible way. It sounds so true then!

But we have all known people who have risen above such temptations. One of the factors was probably because they were secure in their own identity and not threatened—as psychologists would say.

Probably also such people disciplined themselves to think

well of people, to see Christ in them in spite of evident weaknesses, to concentrate on their good qualities, and to rejoice, without jealousy, at their good fortune.

Probably, too, these were people of prayer, and so they became more aware of their own weaknesses and of the mystery of their own delicate psyche.

What could be more wonderful than the descriptive phrase: "I never heard that person utter an unkind word about anyone"?

We can let the judgment to God. He really doesn't need our help for that!

Lent

Prayer while gazing at the cross

Jesus, on our walls there are two kinds of crucifixes: one has your tortured body suspended on it, visible are the crown of thorns and the wounded side; the other shows you with royal priestly robes, with arms outstretched in blessing.

Jesus, which is the true story of your life?

One shows you as poor, destitute, and abandoned; the other shows you in glory.

You are smiling at me, Jesus, because you know I know *theoretically* the answer: you humbled yourself, obediently accepting even death on a cross, and because of this God has highly exalted you and bestowed on you the name above every other name (Phil. 2:8-9).

What you are telling me, Jesus, is that to understand your story I must learn to superimpose one cross on the other.

But you also told me, Jesus, that I must take up my cross daily, that I must die to self and sin, if I wish to share in your glory. How can all that become a reality for me and not mere words, Jesus?

To understand your cross, Jesus, I must further superimpose on it many flashbacks. These I know will help me to understand my daily cross.

First of all, your life was so very consistent. It had direction. Today, Jesus, we would say you had your act together. You came to announce conversion because the kingdom of God was at hand. You resisted the pressures of the crowd, who wanted to make you an earthly king; you resisted the easy solutions proposed by your disciples, who wanted to avoid confrontation and ran scared; you resisted the temptations of the Evil One, who tried to persuade you to give in to immediate glory; you resisted the facile, external show of religious leaders, who sought to impose burdens and not the sweet yoke.

Integrity is the word we would use to describe your character, Lord. You were true to yourself and your destiny; no cheap, easy way for you.

There was no false reasoning in your history to make your Father's will suit your taste. There were no false choices that had to be explained away. You were totally honest with your Father, with yourself, with your disciples, with your persecutors. No wonder death on the cross was the inevitable end as you lived out your mission and your claims.

Jesus, now I see that you had taken up your cross daily. What you preached became your way of life; there was no cheating, no half-measures.

What you were trying to tell us by your life, Jesus, was that each day's cross, carried with integrity, prepares us for those moments of courageous decision-making, when we must place all on the line.

If we have been faithful to self, without deceptive and false reasoning, if we have been honest, open, consistent with others, if we have followed our convictions with the sacrifices they entailed, then we can be sure we have been taking up our crosses daily, and we will become, thus, one with you, Jesus.

Our living, dying, and rising to new life will all become a part of those flashbacks in your own life, Jesus, and become a part of that suffering body on the cross as it is transformed into glory.

31

The desert experience

For the Jewish people, the most memorable and impressive experience of their history—an experience that marked and changed radically their relationship to God—was the Exodus from Egypt and the wandering for forty years in the desert. The desert was not just a place they passed through, but a component in a deep religious experience. That desert experience and its religious and spiritual values became a part of the new covenant, as well.

The desert is not primarily a place of spiritual refuge for uninterrupted solitude. Instead, it is that place where one comes face to face with the unfriendly and overwhelming forces of evil. The struggle for human survival is reduced to its simplest terms. Man's ingenuity is pitted for survival against uncontrollable forces.

Shortly after the six-day war, I was fortunate to have the opportunity to cross the Sinai Desert as a part of a two-jeep convoy going to the Monastery of St. Catherine at the foot of Mount Sinai. We left a camp south of the Suez Canal before sunup. Slashing rains had obscured the paths; the wind was cold and penetrating at first, then raised clouds of dust and destroyed all semblance of path or direction. By sunup it was hot and oppressive. I felt sure that the same experience must be felt by mountain climbers and those adventurous souls who, alone in a barque, face the vast expanses of the ocean. One is alert and every instinct taut.

To the Jewish people, "desert" meant they had as yet no fixed home: they had to wander—tempted frequently to sink their roots and remain immobile at every oasis. What a great temptation when flocks could find pasture and one saw palm trees and succulent fruit! But the Promised Land was beyond. "Desert" did mean deliverance from captivity and slavery to an alien force; it was a path to liberation and freedom.

Most of all, it was that place where one met God. In the desert one had to learn that only God could save. Face to face with those overwhelming hostile forces one had to become aware of his own fragility, fall on two knees and admit his dependence on the God who saves. He alone was the guide to safety. It was also in that desert where God showed his loving kindness and mercy for his people by giving them manna to eat and water to drink. He formed a people, made a covenant of love and hope with them. He became their God; they became his people.

It should be no surprise, then, that the first preaching of the Good News by John the Baptist should be done in a desert setting. And it should be no surprise that Christ began his ministry by spending forty days in the desert. In that way he relived the desert experience of his people. He was tried and tested and tempted, but his victory is significant for us. He triumphed because he relied on God and his word against the powers of evil and the temptations Satan placed in his path. His desert experience was one of struggle, but also one of victory. Later, Christ used terms from the desert experience to show us he is our Savior because he triumphed. He is the new manna, the bread of life: he is the living water; he is the guide, the way, and the light.

The church and each member must pass through that same desert experience. We, too, are a pilgrim church, always tempted to place our confidence in earthly oases, in comfort. We, too, must pass from slavery to freedom from our sins. We, too, must be brought to admit our total dependence on him alone. He is constantly creating of us a new people, fashioned to his likeness.

Lent—a forty-day desert experience—is to remind us of our fragility and our weakness, but also to convert us, change us into people aware of and dependent on God's loving care. Fasting and prayer should bring again to our minds our sinful, weak nature.

But the Christian desert experience had a unique and forever positive element: Christ has conquered death, has triumphed over the forces of evils, and, thus, we are born again

33

into his life. We are resurrection people. We wait during Lent with joyful spiritual hope, knowing that the fruits of Easter are already with us. We know that when the path is obscured by slashing rains or turbulent winds, he is with us as our guide. When we are feeble and frightened, tired of the fight and weary, he is there to refresh us.

Lent reminds us of our weakness and the struggle between evil and good that is waged within us; but Lent also reminds us of God's saving, loving power, of his new life within us. Lent is thus a period of hope and expectation of Easter, just as the whole of Christian living is a hope and an expectation of the fullness of his presence to come.

The mystery of suffering

During the days of Lent and Holy Week the mystery of suffering passes constantly before our eyes. Throughout the whole of the Old Testament holy people struggled with the inconsistency that the good frequently suffered and the evil were often seen to prosper. And then came the scandal of the cross: how Peter refused to believe that Christ should suffer and die!

By his resurrection Jesus gave new meaning to suffering: He did not take it away, but gave it a purpose. Jesus gave meaning not to an abstract suffering, but to my particular, personal suffering. I must die with him to come to new life.

In our day a new view of suffering is so important. So many aspects of our culture tend to avoid the existence of suffering by camouflaging reality. All of the advertisements for medical products give the impression that all pain is rapidly soothed and will pass away. We live under the unrealistic dream that some day science will conquer all pain and find the answers to longevity without suffering.

Let us be realistic. As long as we have physical bodies (and what other kinds are there?), they will tend to deteriorate.

Moreover, we will not be able to select our mode of suffering: something will give way when and in the way we least expect, since we have no control over that vast, complex organism which is our body.

But physical pain is but a portion of true pain. If we are sensitive and caring persons, then we will have the many pains of a more psychological nature that are inevitable if we wish to love and be loved. In fact, the more fully we live and the more intensely we become engaged in life, the more we expose our sensitive natures to suffering: loss of loved ones, suffering with loved ones, being misunderstood, being maligned, not being able to express our sentiments fully and accurately, not communicating, hurting others and being hurt, and so on.

Then there are the added pains that come from our own personality. Perhaps we are not gracious and handsome, perhaps we are less intelligent, perhaps we are timid and feel inadequate, or irascible and offensive, or hypersensitive and easily offended. Perhaps we tend by nature to be depressed. Each one carries the burden that comes with one's personality, one's history. These can be real pains, because they cannot be changed by taking an aspirin. They must be lived through. Attempts to avoid them cause deeper pain and prevent us from living life to its fullest.

What can be the results of sufferings? Sometimes it leads to bitterness. One sees the whole world lined up against one. Everyone else becomes guilty and suspect. Everyone—especially any authority figure—becomes the scapegoat. We exaggerate the defects of others to hide our own, or we become depressed and incapable of facing reality and of real growth. It is so easy to become the turtle and pull into our hard, impregnable shell. In that way, by deadening our sensitivities, we hope to avoid more pain. We close ourselves off to others: we have had enough.

But that is not the Christian way. Our crosses become the means of salvation. As we grow older there is no need to create fictitious crosses. If we are trying to live lives that are full in every human and spiritual way, our crosses will be real and apparent.

Let me mention some of the results that suffering should have on us. First of all, it should make us sensitive to the sufferings of others. Instead of making us bitter and closed, suffering should give us an added awareness of the depth—often hidden—of the sufferings of others. Yes, we cried about having no shoes, till we saw the man with no feet.

Suffering should make us more tenderhearted. Why be ashamed to cry when a beloved one is suffering or dies? (Christ did: remember how he loved Lazarus and suffered with Mary and Martha?) I recall a great-aunt of mine who had lost so many of her children in childbirth or when they were young—one favorite was killed later in the war—but no word of bitterness ever crossed her lips. When one was in her presence, one had that good, comforting feeling of being near someone who understood, who was a shoulder to cry on, with whom few words were needed, whose faith was strong.

We must be convinced that God can work wonders, miracles, through us, precisely because we are weak creatures. That weakness becomes his instrument for doing good. How important it is for priests to understand that! If we, too, are fighting timidity, how gentle we should be to that searching, stammering adolescent who is struggling to express his or her first signs of growing up and must face a cruel and ambiguous world. Those who have suffered to acquire and retain virtue are slow to judge the motives of others.

And then suffering should bring us closer to Christ. If one has not suffered, meditation on the Passion is almost groundless. The more one loves, the deeper one suffers. For this reason Christ's suffering for us was total and our unity in love with him makes his Passion real and complete to us. We understand.

However, during our suffering and during our meditation on Christ's suffering, resurrection is never far away. It becomes redemptive and purifying. Accidentals recede and eternal values come into sharper focus. New life triumphs when one recognizes one's own nothingness and weakness. We rise with Christ with a new hope. St. Benedict put it this way in his Rule:

"Let us share by patience in the sufferings of Christ and thus deserve to have a share also in his kingdom."

Emotional control

As we meditate on the Passion during Lent, we should be impressed by the inner calmness of Jesus in the face of accusations, flogging, and even death. He talked little: short, clear sentences only. From the cross itself he forgives and apologizes for his tormentors: "Lord, forgive them, for they know not what they do."

I suggest that we permit this aspect of Jesus' character and teaching to permeate us a bit more. There is so much need for inner peace and gentleness in the hearts of Christians, even though the world around us seems confused.

One of the great shocks I received on returning to live in the U.S.A. after ten years in Italy came from the manifestations of anger and bitterness that appear in daily American life. It was at times so much more shocking because it came often from older people.

Why are so many Americans angry, bitter people, with so little concern for others? Why are people so irritated and ready to accuse and destroy others?

Americans are tending to become a very litigious people. Everyone is suing or threatening to sue for something. Surely it is not just a desire for money.

We have never had a higher standard of living in our history. We are not engaged in any war. We have never, as a nation, had so many reasons to be thankful and to share with others.

Yet, people are on edge. Read the newspapers, especially the letters to the editors. Sometimes the bitterness and anger tend almost to be vulgar.

Each day I, too, can count on receiving a few such letters. It is true that people have more courage when they write than when they speak, and tend to exaggerate, but still the number of signed and unsigned letters of anger and bitterness, bordering on hate and calumniation, creates a sad picture indeed.

The only remedy is more emotional control and inner peace and calm. For this reason that aspect of Jesus' Passion should be our meditation for Lent.

He did not seek to destroy or condemn or rail at those who persecuted him. He sought to pray for them and forgive.

Most of all, we should not become small-minded people, exaggerating and blowing up little injuries, licking our wounds and seeking redress. It is time to be full of nobility and magnitude and maturity.

"Let your words be for the improvement of others, as occasion offers, and do good to your listeners. . . . Never have grudges against others, or lose your temper, or raise your voice to anybody, or call each other names, or allow any sort of spitefulness.

"Be friends with one another, and kind, forgiving each other as readily as God forgave you in Christ" (Eph. 4:29-32).

Trust

We have always paid special attention to the last words of famous people. In their last message we saw a kind of summation of their lives.

The discourse of Jesus at the Last Supper should be no exception. Here he had gathered those closest to him and gave them the substance of his message. St. John in his gospel records those words, and they remain forever a source for our meditation.

After having predicted Judas' betrayal and Peter's denial of him—events that must have given reason for pessimism, he said to those gathered around him: "Do not let your hearts be troubled. Trust in God still, and trust in me" (Jn. 14:1).

Even in predicting that those around him would desert him, that persecutions would follow, and that the world would hate him, he was able to remain in a spirit of peace and inner tranquility. Even in foreseeing his own death on the cross he preached trust.

His final message was one of trust: Do not be afraid, but trust in God and me.

We all have, like Jesus, so many reasons to be distrustful of others. We have been deceived, tricked, betrayed—often by those we love. We have seen others run scared when we needed support. Perhaps others have also betrayed our confidence, fallen short of the trust we placed in them.

We have never been "betrayed unto death" as Jesus, but perhaps have suffered that kind of neglect, slight, and nonrecognition that Jesus suffered from Peter.

But Jesus tells his disciples, in the face of all such feebleness—to trust. He could have added—and to forgive, just as he forgave Peter totally.

We receive as much trust as we are willing to give to others—no more, no less. If we are suspicious and always attributing low motives to others, if we do not give them occasion to show their love and unselfishness, then we cannot expect to be trusted by others.

To be trusted! How elated and joyful we all feel when someone trusts us, when someone reveals to us some confidence—especially if it leaves the other vulnerable and weak before us. They trust because they know our love will never harm nor destroy them.

How Jesus must have trusted Peter and John and Thomas and even Judas! He gave the fullness of his message, of his love to them. Then he told them not to be afraid, but to trust in him.

Few people really learn to trust totally. All hold back a bit—out of fear of losing total independency. But trust means we realize that someone's love for us is so great that he or she would never do harm to us—only good.

Jesus is calling out to us to trust him. That is what prayer is all about—returning that trust.

We are not afraid to be weak and vulnerable before him, because he loves us.

We are not afraid to reveal our fears, because he stands to support us.

We are not afraid to express our uneasiness to move ahead in life and face the future, because he is with us.

"Do not be afraid," he calls out. "Trust me."

Jesus, let me learn to trust you totally and completely— without reserve. More than that, teach me not to be afraid to trust others.

As you trusted weak Peter and doubting Thomas, as you forgave their weakness and continued to trust, so teach me to trust and accept the weakness in the love of others, so they, too, can learn to trust.

Teach me not to be afraid: You are with me still. You trust me. You forgive me. I will trust. I will be trusted. I will not be afraid.

Being alone

We are all a bit shocked when Mark places on Jesus' lips the words of the psalmist: "My God, my God, why have you forsaken me?" (Psalm 22:2). Jesus seems totally abandoned as he hangs there on the cross (Mk. 15:34). And yet, during his life we find him often alone, from the first temptations at the beginning of his ministry (Lk. 4) till the agony in the garden (Lk. 22).

Somehow we have come to believe, however, that being alone is the same as being lonely, and, thus, an evil to be exterminated. There are so many lonely people around us. Their lives seem empty, unfulfilled; they are desolate, forgotten, marginal, unappreciated.

There are so many people who cannot or will not relate to others. Sometimes they seem frightened, most of the time just neglected. Everyone is too busy to bother.

In every one of us there is this tendency toward loneliness. No one seems really to understand us. (Often we don't understand ourselves!) Others always fall short of what we expect of them. They fail to notice when we are hurting or pass off as insignificant something which has affected us deeply.

Our society, they tell us, produces an overabundance of lonely people (the "lonely crowd")! The anonymity that comes from size, urbanization, the workaholic instinct, competitiveness, the desire to get ahead, causes some to be trampled under and left behind. But it is often hard to tell which—the achiever or the "marginated"—is the more lonely.

The elderly have a special problem in our society. They seem to serve no practical, useful purpose; no one seems interested in hearing stories about "the good old days." People live longer, but still there is the inevitable experience of seeing so many loved ones die off. The group of those who care gets smaller.

What solutions are proposed?

Some young—and not so young, too!—seem to find their solution in gregariousness and in filling the silence with continuous noise. Carry a transistor with you and you are not alone, they seem to say!

Some good-willed people try to invade that loneliness by forcing all kinds of sharing, by "raping" others' privacy, by invading and exposing till the lonely are exhausted and dispossessed of self.

If we read on in Psalm 22, we find the psalmist treating his own loneliness in a different way: "But you, O Lord," he says, "be not far from me: O my help, hasten to aid me" (v. 20).

Part of the solution for the lonely must be, certainly, to gain confidence and trust in others who care; but the other half of the solution has to be turning loneliness into solitude.

Solitude is not loneliness, although both mean being alone. Solitude means being alone to be oneself and to be alone with God. It means a lack of noise and distraction, but the inner silence does not lead to emptiness. It means time to listen, to "re-collect" oneself, to let God's presence take hold. It means time and quietude to think things out and not be propelled along without reflection. It means time to pray.

We have to learn, too, to respect the solitude of others; we have to know when they need to be alone.

We say a novice has to learn to keep his cell, he cannot be constantly roaming the hallways looking for distractions.

There must be some point, deep within oneself, where everybody is really alone, where no one else can penetrate, where all sharing and descriptions of how we feel seem empty. But at that moment we can be the most full, because it is then that God takes hold of us.

Being human means accepting the imperfection of not being able to share totally until we are all one in him. "Father, into thy hands I commend my spirit."

Prayers

Prayer on a rainy morning

Jesus, I am a nervous wreck this morning. Sleep did not come easily. Just too much on my mind, and no answers in sight.

Did you have sleepless nights, Jesus, worrying about whether Peter or John would hold up under the pressures you had subjected them to? Or whether Judas' bitterness could have been avoided with more fraternal treatment?

Your problems seem, on second thought, a bit like my own.

But you didn't have committee meetings! Or are those gatherings of your disciples described in Luke 9 and 10, before they were sent out on mission and again after they returned, really the first recorded meetings? But, then, those meetings were about how to preach the Gospel and about sharing Faith experiences.

Today there will be several meetings. Will I be peevish and impatient? Teach me, Jesus, at those meetings to seek your will, to worry about how to preach the gospel and to share faith. It could well be that all present will forget to speak for your point of view, if I am remiss.

Were you afraid, Jesus, of making a mistake, of misjudg-

43

ing people or a situation? Maybe not, but I am sure, for example, that the sad consequences must have flashed through your mind when you asked that rich young man to follow you and he did not. Why did you do it? To give him the chance.

Were you impatient with others, Jesus? You have to admit that you were a bit violent in your choice of words toward hypocrites and those money changers. On the other hand, how you held your cool when you stood before Pilate and were so crazily accused!

Jesus, help me to keep my cool when I have to face people who disagree with me, when I am misquoted, when I make mistakes. I never know when I am defending my own position through pride or when I am truly defending your messsage. Help me on that score, too.

Teach me to make decisions and accept their consequences, but to have the courage to recognize when I goof and to admit it. Help me to grow today, Jesus, from all those mistakes I am sure to make.

But it is not fair to you, Jesus, to end this talking on such a peevish tone. So . . .

I thank you for the light of this day. Although it is still dim, I know it will grow brighter and brighter. Let my life today be the same. Will you help me see those dark moments as sources of still hidden, unrevealed light that is waiting to be released?

Jesus, I thank you for this air. As it slowly enters the lungs, purifies, and then is exhaled, I sense that today your Spirit will fill my being and cleanse it. Jesus, I thank you for this day. Who cares how many meetings there will be or how many decisions?

It is another day to be with you, another day to hear you tell us of your Gospel, another day to be sent on your mission, another day to share faith with other people.

Oh, yes, and another day to make mistakes.

So, I know I will be coming back tonight, Jesus, with another shopping list of questions and worries—and sentiments of gratitude.

I don't want to sound irreverent, but have a good day,
Jesus. I know I will.

Prayer on a rainy day

Jesus, why did you have to be born outside the warmth of
a normal home and in a region not your own? Why did you
have to die outside the city? Probably you accepted to be born
and to die "detached" so we could freely seek you out and make
the journey to you on our own.

With the shepherds and the kings, the poor and the rich,
the lowly and the noble, we are all equal in our search for you.
No one has the advantage. Your equal love for all is the source
of our equality.

With the good thief, with Mary and John, we also can be
with you on Calvary—if we have the courage.

Jesus, thank you for making your life a new crossroads
where every human being can pass by.

*   *   *

Jesus, if you are God, why did you come into our history
so slowly? You could have flashed across the heavens or
scorched the earth with your fire. But you came so quietly and
grew up and wandered on foot and ate what was given to you
and had no place of your own. You came at a human pace for
our comfort.

If at times we seem irritated, even now, that your pace is
too slow, help us to remember that you are accommodating us.
(O, that church you founded is also so slow; but we know that
not all can run as fast as John: he outstripped Peter to the
tomb—and waited.)

We say thanks for your slow pace—but not without
difficulty; it would be so much easier if you came with fire and
hurricanes. But then it wouldn't be you—gentle and loving.

45

*   *   *

If you are God, Jesus, why did you select a Judas among your closest collaborators, or even a Peter who ran scared? Were you trying to tell us that you could build your kingdom in spite of our weaknesses? You seemed more concerned about changing people's hearts than organizational success. You taught conversion away from earthly ways of thinking: you focused on yourself as the way, the truth, and the life.

Peter and Judas—they both strayed: but Peter cried and came back. There is no despair in Peter, just contrition and conversion. But he was not alone when he fell asleep in the garden as you suffered; we were all with him.

Why, Jesus, have we so often lost a sense of sin and of offending you? Why do our sensitivities fall asleep in your presence? We are sure of your love and forgiveness, but can we be so callous toward your commands? "If you love me, you will keep my commandments." Teach us what that kind of love is all about. It led you to give up your life for us. In our weaknesses, how can we ever imitate such an example? We are such sleepy and dull creatures. "Slowly, Lord, with us," we are saying, "not too fast in your demands." And just a minute ago, Jesus, we complained that it was you who were too slow. We are grateful for giving us time.

*   *   *

Why, too, Jesus, did you cry when Lazarus died? They must have been close friends of yours—Mary, Martha, and Lazarus. How do we enter into that circle of friendship? By offering you hospitality? By believing in you? Would you stop for a meal at our house?

You are smiling. You thought of all of us before you left this earth. You offer a banquet beyond human imagination as a sign, a pledge, of your love: "Take and eat; this is my body." Sorry, Jesus, we are so used to being fed by your manna; we forgot.

Are you also crying with us in our sorrows today? Are you willing to raise us from the dead? Yes, we know you no longer call us strangers but friends; we are thankful for friendship.

*   *   *

Why, Jesus, did you love children so? Why did you say we had to become childlike to understand you? Are you trying to teach us to approach you in a simple way, without affectation, without "big" ideas? Children are attracted to people who are kind and generous and loving toward them. How easily they recognize insincerity and sham!

But we are to imitate both you and children. Simple in approaching you, loving and generous and kind toward others—that must be our double program.

It is so much easier, Jesus, to defend rights and carry placards than to be kind and loving and simple and childlike. Teach us to be your kind of hero; and thanks for cutting us down to size.

*   *   *

We have so many "if's" and "why's" to ask about; but they all end up in the mystery of your love for us finite and vacillating creatures, a love which impelled you to enter our history, to become one like us and to share our human plight. You continue to have that same care and concern today for all of us. You are still entering our lives daily.

If at times, Lord Jesus, we seem ungrateful, it is our sleepiness, our thoughtlessness, our over-preoccupation with our job, our work, our burdens. Help us to make you a part of them each day. That's friendship.

Thanks, Jesus, for being one of us, so we can be one with you and your Father with your Holy Spirit. It is good to be alive—in you. (But I still have many "if's" and "why's" to ask you about when we get to know each other better.)

Prayer on a rainy evening

Jesus, where were you today?

Were you in the vague glimpse of sustaining hope that helped me face the depressing feeling that it was useless to try to touch that hardened, frightened heart?

Were you the fullness of love behind those few occasions of receiving and giving comforting help?

Were you in the sudden flash of light that seemed to penetrate those moments of frustration where all signs of human success had vanished?

Were you the fullness of joy behind that smiling, toothless child who grasped my hand at church?

Were you in that glimmer of patience to endure serenely my inability to find a solution to that vexing, complicated situation?

Were you the fullness of beauty behind the Mozart Symphony that was interrupted by the squealing telephone?

Were you in the silence of those youngsters who could not express themselves and were so awkward and ill at ease, but still wanted to be near?

Were you in the disfiguring, physical pain on that young face that looked so mysteriously at me and made me aware of my own cheap comfort?

Were you in that exhilarating freedom as I walked along the shore and looked out at the sailboats and let the breeze clear out those cobwebbed ideas?

Were you in the peace and contentment of the old nun's wrinkled face and in those deep-sunk eyes that peered up and asked for help, though no sound came from her throat?

Were you in that expression of human trust when that young agitated mother whispered she had cancer and wanted a blessing?

Were you in those words of thanks, hastily spoken lest they show weakness or dependency, when one would have expected from a grown man strength and self-assurance.

How many times did you speak to me today, Lord?

It is more difficult to find you in those tedious hours in the car, in that endless chitchat, in those bitter complaining letters, in that balance sheet. But you must have been there, just as you were in the sunrise and flowers, and, of course, at Mass, and in those more exciting and striking events.

You were in my heart, too.

The problem, Lord, is that it takes a rainy evening and a bit of internal silence to bring each event into focus and to find you there.

Prayer on a foggy day

Today, dear Lord Jesus, during this meeting of all the bishops of the U.S.A., I am reminded more than ever of my duties as a bishop.

One bishop this morning recalled to us a famous passage St. Augustine addrssed to his flock. He said to them: "When I am frightened by what I am to you, then I am consoled by what I am with you. To you, I am the bishop; with you, I am a Christian. The first is an office, the second a grace; the first a danger, the second salvation."

All of the tasks of a bishop frighten me this morning, dear Jesus—perhaps because it is rainy and dreary out, perhaps because our meetings seem to touch lightly on a thousand aspects of the church in the U.S. today and we hesitate to scratch deeply for fear of not being able to put it all back together.

Perhaps, however, it is all a bit simpler to analyze: perhaps I just sense that people expect too much of me. They cry out for spiritual leadership, when I am just struggling to keep head above water. They expect me to be a model of kindness and patience, and I become easily irritated and impatient. They expect me to be an example of prayer, and this morning, Lord, my mind is distracted and foggy like the weather.

They expect me to inspire each time I open my mouth or to have new and striking insights in every discussion. They believe I can talk on any subject at any time without preparation. They believe they can program me like a machine.

Surely, Lord, they don't think I have the stamina of Pope John Paul II, or the pastoral touch of John Paul I, or the sharp intellect of Paul VI, or the mellow, paternal heart of John XXIII. What models, Lord, you have given them to match me against!

Then there are the many wounds out there to be healed, and I am reaching so very few. How many have been "turned off" by the church and its lifestyle! How many have been hurt by caustic words or signs of coldness! How many are bitter because no one seemed to care when they were in need or in grief!

But, Lord, even if you gave me a 30 hour day and all the stamina of John Paul II, and all the pastoral insights of John Paul I, and all the intellectual reflections of Paul II, and all the warmth and kindness of John XXIII, still it would not be enough.

What a foggy morning, Lord!

Help me to see that it really does not all depend on me. I guess it will always remain foggy, until I can see more clearly what I am "with you, Lord," and what I am "with them": grace, a Christian, salvation, consolation.

I keep forgetting, Lord: the kingdom is yours. The flock is yours and you can do without me. You can do more with me than I could ever do myself. You have the calculator, I just punch keys.

You are the source of hope and consolation and salvation: I am but the conduit.

With your flock, I am one who has been touched by your love and brought to the saving water. I am one with them in that baptismal water.

I was not sent alone, but with them, Lord, with your chosen ones—that royal priesthood, your people.

Of course, we become discouraged and foggy when we think we can do it alone. Being sent is a part of being Christian: you made that clear, Jesus, before you left this earth.

My episcopal ministry is to minister to the baptismal ministry of others which I also share. It is so complicated, Lord—but consoling.

And so, I can thank you for the fog this morning. It made me realize, Lord, how much depends on you and how much we Christians, bishops or not, depend on each other.

Take care of your people, Lord!

God's Word Stretches Me

Prejudice

In my little hometown in Pennsylvania there were no black people. As a child, the only blacks I ever saw were the "honey-dippers." A couple of times a year they would come through the back alley with their suction pumps to clean out the outhouses. Then they would sprinkle white lime all over the place—and themselves, too.

We would follow respectfully at a distance, full of curiosity, but never with enough courage to say a word.

Even in my high school and seminary years I lived in a totally white society. Finally, as a young priest, I went to New York to study and formed my first friendships with blacks at Juilliard. I had so much to learn, because unconsciously I had formed stereotypes in my mind that had to be broken down.

Then, years later, when I went to Africa, the opposite experience came my way. I didn't know how to handle being a stereotype, that is, identified with the money-conscious, gum chewing, soft American. How often I felt like screaming out and yelling—"But that's not me!"

In South America, too, I couldn't understand why people did not accept me as me, instead of thinking of me immediately as a greedy, insensitive "capitalist."

*　　*　　*

Among my friends at Columbia University was a young Jewish couple—he was a brilliant psychiatrist, she was a capable musician. They had a beautiful young child of five named Cammie. Cammie had inherited her father's brains and her mother's musical instinct.

The parents were desirous that Cammie grow up without prejudices; but in the area of the city where they lived there were no blacks. Knowing how much the little girl loved the music of Nat King Cole, they felt the time had come to confront the racial issue.

One Sunday they invited me to their apartment for the Ed Sullivan Show on which Nat King Cole would be a guest star. Cammie would be allowed to stay up to watch the show.

All was carefully prepared, including the speech of the psychiatrist-father for the right moment.

Then came Nat King Cole. Little Cammie, sitting on her tiny stool close to the screen, watched enthralled for a bit, then turned to her father and said, hesitatingly, "Daddy, something's the matter. It's not what I expected."

The eager response came back, "Tell me, Cammie, what's wrong. What didn't you expect?"

"He doesn't look like I expected," the little girl said in a disappointed tone.

"But what's the matter, Cammie?"

"Why isn't he wearing his crown, if they call him King?"

The evening passed and she never noticed the skin.

Prejudices are not innate. We are not born with them. We and our culture create them and keep them alive. We transmit them.

*　　*　　*

What prejudices did Jesus have to overcome?

He called Matthew, a tax collector, to be among his

53

disciples. He even sat at table with that despised class.

He talked with the Samaritan woman at the well and was willing to drink from her "unclean" pail.

Most of all, he had to reject ideas about himself. The Jews wanted him to play a role. They wanted to make him their type of king. His own disciples—Peter included—had a false image into which they wanted to cast him. They couldn't understand why he had to suffer.

His message, too, leaves no place for prejudice. He comes to save all. Each person is precious in his eyes; each person is the object of his love.

The kingdom belongs to all.

*   *   *

Bishop Helder-Camara once told me he could reduce to a few sentences the ideals that guide his life. One of these is the equal worth and dignity of every living person on this earth.

Why? Because that is how it is in God's eyes. That is how it must become in our own.

The greatest miracle of all

It is easy to believe in miracles if one believes in God. Our concept of God includes the belief that "nothing is hard or impossible to him." If God created nature a certain way, why can he not be free to alter or suspend its laws as he wishes?

Perhaps our problem today is not that people don't believe in miracles, but that they turn religion into a search for the miraculous, rather than for holiness. Miracles are not the end, the scope, of religion.

Miracles in the gospel message are a support system. They are signs of God's power to save and redeem us.

For this reason we must look beyond those miracles to belief in the God who loves us and to the hope that he will continue to help us face this real world. That faith and hope, then, find their expression in actions on our part that imitate Jesus' love for others.

We must resist the temptation of that generation which Jesus condemned because they sought only signs and wonders, and thus missed the greatest wonder of all, the miracle of our redemption.

Jesus was faced at the beginning of his public ministry with a similar temptation. He could have permitted his reputation to become that of an extraordinary faith-healer; he could have allowed the excessive curiosity of the crowd to rest on his powers to perform miracles rather than on his message of salvation.

In Chapter 4 of St. Luke's account of the beginning of Jesus' mission in Galilee, we hear of the numerous miracles he had performed. Luke tells us about the cure of the man possessed of an unclean spirit; he recounts the story of the healing of Simon's mother-in-law from a burning fever. Jesus laid hands on all and cured them.

But at the end of that chapter we find him seeking out a lonely place to be with his Father and to sort out his thoughts—and his mission. When the crowds caught up with him and tried to prevent him from leaving them—every town would like to have its own faith-healer and miracle-worker— he resisted this temptation, took the attention away from the miracles and placed the emphasis on the message he was preaching.

"I must proclaim," he said, "the Good News of the kingdom of God to the other towns too, because that is what I was sent to do."

God did not create the universe in a particular way just to suspend its laws for our amusement or for tickling our curiosity. He will not permit us to turn him into a substitute for doctors, physicists, or psychiatrists. We must not make him into a "Houdini."

He will transform us from within, if we listen to his

message and live by it. He will transform our faith-community in the same way.

When we all become loving, caring human beings, as he was, that will be the greatest and the only important miracle.

Friendship

It seems to me that when I was younger, quotes about friendship were found more often in the literature we read in school and in our public magazines than are found today. More plaques extolling friendship were found hanging on our walls.

Passages such as these from the Book of Sirach were cited often: "A faithful friend is a sturdy shelter; he who finds one finds a treasure."—"A faithful friend is beyond price, no sum can balance his worth."—"A faithful friend is a life-saving remedy, such as he who fears God finds."

We all recall how such passages from the poets were a part of our grade school repertoire. Is there anyone who did not cite Kahlil Gibran at that time?

Why is it that today such odes in praise of friendship seem to have disappeared? Friendship is seldom talked about and less often praised? Why?

Do we consider such words all too sentimental? Have the amateur Freudian pop-analysts so cowed us with their jargon that we are afraid to admit friendship?

Or, perhaps it is just that we do not really prize friendship in our society. It could well be that we have become too cynical, too critical, too selfish for friendship. We lack the kind of trust on which friendship can be based. We remember too readily the sayings about the boon companions who disappear in time of trouble.

Friendship also takes time. We have all grown selfish and lack the leisure for just being with people. Friendships are born of leisure. We also lack the openness to other ways of life and thinking, other cultures, other backgrounds, other tastes and interests that make friendships rich and rewarding.

Our mobile society is not made for cultivating lasting friendships.

And yet, Jesus called his apostles friends. "This is my commandment: love one another as I have loved you. . . . You are my friends if you do what I command you. . . . I no longer speak of you as slaves . . . instead I call you friends" (Jn. 15:12-15).

The word Jesus chose to use to express his love for his closest apostles was thus "friends." Friendship must be then a holy and important relationship. Jesus is not given to sentimentality and he uses titles very sparingly.

If we have not learned how to spend time with others, be open to receiving them as they are and with the special gifts they have to share, how can we be prepared to spend time with Jesus? If we do not trust others and find time for them, will we find time for Jesus?

Friendship with Jesus is not a substitute for the lack of closeness to others, but is the culmination of a lifestyle that enjoys sharing, trusting, and communicating with others.

And Jesus is never jealous. He is always happy to be a member of the friendship circle. He always uses the word in the plural.

His friendship, too, must be cultivated with leisure and time for sharing.

The little people

How easy it is for faith to become abstract and disembodied, especially in the hands of us priests. Too often we expect of the laity a kind of active Christian life that is possible only for the young and independent or the old and retired. We expect full participation in the life of the community and

57

abstract from the daily family existence.

Most people, instead, are taken up with a thousand very real problems that absorb their time and concern: how to find a job that will last and bring in enough money to support a growing family; how to find the means of giving a good Christian education to each child—grade school, high school, college (if ends meet); how to pay for new glasses, braces for a child's teeth, and car insurance and tennis shoes and hairdos....

We priests can plead with the bishop if the group we are living with becomes incompatible and ask for a transfer or seek other living arrangements. But how many families have to face each day the problems of close quarters, growing irritabilities, aloof and incommunicative teen-agers, interfering grandparents, crying babies?

Our sphere of activity leaves more room for initiative than many imagine. Most priests are able to evolve their apostolate as they wish, preach the kind of sermons they choose, conduct the liturgy with a knowledge that they are still in command. But how many people must work at jobs they dislike, because they need the income? How many must endure arrogant and empty-headed bosses? How many work under circumstances that are subhuman, because they fear a complaint would lead to their dismissal?

It is gratifying and gives meaning to life to work for the kingdom of God and to try to help people. What would it be like to spend hours daily selling ice cream to pampered children, or looking all day at numbers that represent other people's money, or trying to evolve a better disinfectant?

(The priest's life is not all rosy; but he has a different set of frustrations and hardships.)

Each time, however, I rise to preach, I realize I live in a hothouse. The real world is where there are crying babies, mouths to be fed, uninspiring jobs to be filled.

The moments most people can spare for coming together to celebrate the liturgy with others becomes then most precious, almost a luxury. That prayer must help give meaning to the daily routine and show how all that monotony is of concern to God.

How can these sacred moments encourage people to grow as Christians during all the tedious, tough times? Most of all, I guess, it is our task as priests to help sustain a vision: there is a God who loves and cares, the one who sent Jesus. He expects all of us to love and care, too. We must point out to others that the little signs of caring they receive should be seen as signs of God's concern; they, in turn, must show others through their own loving kindness that God cares. In this way the vision is nurtured and sustained.

The little concerns of our daily lives are God's concern.

Is that why Jesus lived and worked thirty years in a carpenter's family in preparation for only three years of preaching?

Now I know how it was that he understood the problems of the little people.

Blest are you poor

Have you ever asked yourself why Jesus preferred the poor and the destitute? Why is the first of the Beatitudes: "Blest are you poor; the reign of God is yours" (Lk. 6:20)? (Notice that in Luke, unlike the same passage in Matthew 5:3, the phrase is not softened to read "poor in spirit," but is left in its starker form.)

The theme of the first recorded sermon that Jesus preached centered on the truth that the prophecy of Isaiah, Chapter 61, was realized in himself: "The spirit of the Lord is upon me; therefore he has anointed me. He has sent me to bring glad tidings to the poor, to proclaim liberty to captives, recovery of sight to the blind and release to prisoners" (Lk. 4:18). The scene was his hometown of Nazareth.

Luke's gospel records so many of Jesus' teachings on the dangers of riches. It is a refrain that is never far from earshot.

Chapter 12 relates the parable about the rich man who wanted to build larger and larger grain bins with more and more reserves. "You fool! This very night your life shall be required of you. To whom will all this piled-up wealth of yours go?" (Lk. 12:20).

Everyone knows the teaching that follows on the lilies of the field and God's providence. Instead of being anxious and concerned about food and clothing, Jesus tells us: "Seek instead the Father's kingship over you, and the rest will follow in turn" (Lk. 12:31).

If you have a dinner, do not invite the wealthy, but the beggars, the crippled, the lame, the blind, because they cannot repay you (Lk. 14:12). "You cannot give yourself to God and money" (Lk. 16:13).

In Chapter 16 one finds the story of the rich man, dressed in purple and linen, who feasted splendidly each day, and the beggar named Lazarus (Lk. 16:19-31). After death it was Lazarus who rested in Abraham's bosom. The rich man kept calling out to Abraham to send Lazarus to bring him at least a few drops of water, but Abraham answered: "Between you and us there is fixed a great abyss."

In Chapter 18 Jesus discusses with the rich young man what he must do to share in everlasting life. When Jesus tells him to sell all he has and give it to the poor, and then to follow him, "he grew melancholy, for he was a very rich man" (Lk. 18:23). Jesus observed: "How hard it will be for the rich to go into the kingdom of God" (Lk. 18:24).

But the early church had to fight also against the "welfare" syndrome. There were those at Thessalonica who refused to work: they were waiting for the end of the world to come soon (2 Thess. 3:6-15). "Indeed, when we were with you," writes Paul to them, "we used to lay down the rule that anyone who would not work should not eat" (2 Thess. 3:10). The servant who did not put his money out on loan and see to it that it was productive for his master was punished (Lk. 19:11-27). Paul boasted that he worked for his own support and was not a burden on anyone (2 Thess. 3:7-8). Jesus' preaching was not to be an excuse for laziness.

The passages of the gospel on riches, however, disturb many. But they will not go away: they are integral to the whole of Jesus' mission. Yet they do seem so contrary to the American social standards which count success by the wealth one has piled up. As a boy, I heard so often about the Carnegies or the Mellons or the Rockefellers. From rags to riches was the theme of so many novels or movies—the Horatio Alger theme.

Have we worked out in our lives these demands of the gospel? Although no one would perhaps say that he or she seeks "salvation" in wealth, nevertheless, the temptation to water down or ignore the gospel message on the danger of riches is always present.

If Jesus warns of the dangers of riches and seems to favor the poor, it was because the latter were so much more disposed to hear his message. They knew they needed help and were open to change. The rich, on the other hand, tend to be contented with the way things are and frightened of any alteration of the *status quo*.

As Jesus pointed out, riches can tend to weaken our faith and trust in God's providence. It is so easy to forget that God is a provident father, concerned about each of us, and to remember his goodness only "if nothing else works." Anxiety grows stronger as one accumulates wealth: it does not decrease. Total security is never reached, so one searches always for more.

Because of its all-absorbing nature, concern for riches and wealth prevents one from recognizing and seeing the real issues of life—those which really count. Concern and anxiety and greed cloud one's judgment and limit one's vision.

But perhaps the greatest danger of riches is that they can *buy people*. People can be so easily seen as means of serving me, since I have the money to pay. In Luke 16 the rich man, even after death, did not see the beggar Lazarus as a real person, but continued to consider him as one made to serve himself—to bring water, to take a message.

The poor are those who realize the frailty of human nature, the precariousness of all success in human terms. At the same time they have a deep trust in God's goodness, his love, his concern, his mercy.

The poor of the gospel see food and clothing as *means*, not an end in themselves. Most of all, they are detached and able to use goods properly, because they are seeking God's service, his kingdom, above all else.

The poor are those who can wager all for God: they can "hang loose." And, above all, they know how to pray, because they have experienced the marvels God can do for the lowly. Like Mary, they are full of joy in God, their Savior, and can proclaim his greatness (Lk. 1:46-47).

"Blest are you poor; the reign of God is yours."

The Good Shepherd

The theme of the Good Shepherd is an excellent one for reflection for all of us.

Perhaps the greatest revelation in the New Testament is found in the parable of the Prodigal Son and in Jesus' parable of the Good Shepherd. These two images alter totally our concept of God and our relationship to him.

No longer is God seen as wrathful, or distant, or quick to punish, but, rather, he is seen as one who truly forgives and cares for each one of us, even when we are helpless and weak and have abandoned his household.

Perhaps to us of the twentieth century the image of the shepherd seems less clear, because we are not, for the most part, an agrarian people who have had experience with sheep. Sheep are the most helpless of creatures. We all have heard of the meekness of the lamb. For this reason the shepherd had to be constantly on the watch to protect his flock. Each night, all the shepherds would gather their sheep into a common corral and one would always stand watch while the others slept. Naturally, some foul play would take place during the night, so that some sheep would get "lost." Jesus talks also about such shepherds.

Then, in the morning, each shepherd standing outside the corral would call his sheep, and his own, recognizing his voice, would follow him. He, of course, had numbered them and would recall when one was missing. He would go in search of each lost one.

In saying that he is the Good Shepherd, Jesus wanted us to know that he "recognizes" each one of us. He cares for each one of us and wishes to be part of our trials and problems. This is indeed a new and consoling revelation.

But Jesus goes even further in his description of the Good Shepherd. The Good Shepherd lays down his life for his sheep. This means that he is willing to make any sacrifice so that his flock will be intact, so that all the sheep will be safe and none will be lost. In saying that he will lay down his life for his sheep, he is telling us that he is willing to suffer death on the cross for our salvation.

Perhaps to most of us this model or parable seems a bit unflattering. We feel that we are identified with the helpless and unprotected lambs. Perhaps, for this reason, we miss the point. The goal of our Christian life is really to imitate Jesus: He must be our model. For this reason we must imitate the Good Shepherd—not the helpless sheep.

What this means in the concrete is that we must be concerned about others, the unprotected. We must be willing to give up our lives, if necessary, and to sacrifice and to endure hardships for the sake of those who are unable to protect themselves.

Each one of us—not just those in authority—is expected to imitate Jesus as Good Shepherd in serving and helping those in need.

Easter

Marana tha! Come, Lord, Jesus, come!

"Marana tha! Come, Lord Jesus, come!"

We live in the "in-between times." Jesus is risen; he is indeed with us till the end of time as he promised. Yet he is constantly coming, constantly entering again our lives, so that the fullness of his presence is not yet ours. Therefore, we must pray:

"Marana tha! Come, Lord Jesus, come!"

We know that Jesus is with us now in that most extraordinary way, sacramentally and really, in the Eucharist. We enjoy that presence; we are strengthened by it. Through it or in it we are all united, too, to him and to each other; but we also know that the Mass is but a pledge, a foretaste, a preview of the fullness of his presence. Therefore, we must pray:

"Marana tha! Come, Lord Jesus, come!"

We know that Jesus sent us his Spirit, the Spirit of understanding and light, of courage and consolation. We know that his Spirit abides in the church and in us and is a vital partner in our own lives. Yet it is often a struggle to discern where that Spirit is present. The Spirit of Jesus has trouble penetrating our sinful selfishness. Therefore, we must pray:

"Marana tha! Come, Lord Jesus, come!"

64

We know we can find the presence of Jesus in the poor and the helpless. He told us so. We will indeed be judged by our response to his presence in the needy. But we continue to see only ourselves and not others in need. Therefore, we must pray:

"Marana tha! Come, Lord Jesus, come!"

We have heard often the texts of Isaiah and Jeremiah about the peace and justice that will reign when the Messianic age has come. But Matthew reminds us that we must still be constantly seeking that kingdom, a kingdom of peace and justice, of love and happiness. We seem so far from realizing such a kingdom. Therefore, we must pray:

"Marana tha! Come, Lord Jesus, come!"

At times, while we are at prayer, in the silence of our inmost being, we sense his presence of love and care. But at other times distractions and the heaviness of our hearts stand in the way. We realize how much there is to be done to conform our ways to his. Therefore, we must pray:

"Marana tha! Come, Lord Jesus, come!"

In times of joy and happiness we think that he is near because all is well. But such moments are passing and fleeting and fragile. We know he is also in the darker moments, the times when the cross seems to dominate over resurrection. In all such moments we must pray:

"Marana tha! Come, Lord Jesus, come!"

We know that Jesus is present in and works through everyone, but especially through his bishops, priests, and deacons, since they have been ordained to serve his people as he did. They have a unique relationship to his presence and to the new life—his life—he brings his people. For this reason, united as one body, one community of Faith, we pray:

"Marana tha! Come, Lord Jesus, come!"

Life in the Risen Lord

During the Easter Season Jesus' last discourse to his

disciples forms the core of our liturgical readings. How is the Risen Lord with us now? What are the consequences of our baptism into his life and death?

We know that our personal history and the history of the world have been changed because of his Resurrection. We, too, the Church tells us, walk in newness of life. We must live in him as he lives in us. His life, though, was a life of love and service, because he emptied himself of his glory to be one like us and he came to serve that we, too, might have newness of life—abundantly.

Life, then, to us Christians can never be a cheap commodity. Our prophetic witness as baptized people is to safeguard that sanctity of life in all its aspects.

For our witness to be credible, though, we must do more than preach. We witness by our whole lifestyle; it must say to others that we value human life in all its aspects as precious in the sight of the Lord.

Our lifestyle must become like his: he came as our brother to redeem, to save, to heal us; he came for the poor, the defenseless, the sick, the lame. "Being rich, he became poor for us, so that he might enrich us by his poverty."

Jesus was the Messiah of the poor: Blessed are the poor in spirit. He was the Messiah of the peacemakers and the nonviolent: Blessed are those who suffer persecution for justice' sake.

The image the gospel portrays of Jesus is that of caring, curing, healing, encouraging: in other words, he is concerned about the quality of life and takes special care with those whose lives seem worthless. At the final judgment he will not ask: Were you an archbishop? Did you talk in tongues? But, rather: Did you feed the hungry, clothe the naked, visit the sick, and so on.

It becomes then the duty of every Christian to be concerned about the quality of life here on this planet. It is our duty to defend human beings against anything that would degrade or lessen their worth.

All must be the object of our concern—from the unborn to the aged. The most defenseless are, of course, the not-yet-born. Yes, they are objects of God's special love, and they must be the objects of our love and concern, too. The astonishing rise in the number of abortions in the U.S.A. should frighten all of us. Has life become so cheap?

If we want our anti-abortion thrust to be credible, however, we must show by word and act that it extends to the whole of life.

First, we must welcome with joy the birth of another person, one to share in Jesus' life, one loved by him and to be loved by us. We must love children.

We must be concerned that all, poor or rich, physically endowed or handicapped, receive the means of developing fully who they are. When we read that over a third of this world lives in subhuman conditions, some in our own inner city, when we read of starvation in Africa, India, here and elsewhere, we must become a part of those movements that try to reverse such inequality. Again, this must be done, not just by words, but in our lifestyle. Only then will our witness be credible.

Most of all, we must love life ourselves. That does not mean that we seek only pleasure, but, rather, that our attitudes toward life and toward others are positive and caring. The quality of our own lives will be measured by our desire to serve and share, by our joy to learn and love, by our eagerness to form friendships, by our openness to the young, by our willingness to sit at the feet of the old.

For those of you who have not yet read Pope John Paul's encyclical, *Redemptor Hominis*, I would advise you to do so. Because of it, he will be regarded in history as the true prophet in our day of the dignity and worth of each human person. In it he shows again and again how the basis for love of life and for human worth and dignity come from the incarnation, from Jesus as redeemer of all mankind.

Let this sample whet your interest. "Human nature, by the

very fact that it was assumed, not absorbed by him, has been raised in us also to a dignity beyond compare. For, by his incarnation, he, the Son of God, in a certain way united himself with each human being. He worked with human hands, he thought with a human mind. He acted with a human will, and with a human heart he loved. Born of the Virgin Mary, he has truly been made one of us, like us in all things except sin, he, the redeemer of the human race."

Fullness of life

Jesus came that we might have fullness of life. There must, then, be some relationship between the Good News of the gospel and human growth.

Pope John Paul touches on this theme in his encyclical, *Redemptor Hominis*. One passage struck me in particular. In describing our way of sharing in the "kingly service" of Jesus, he shows that we can attain to "being kings" by collaborating with the grace Jesus has gained for us and thus produce in each one of us a mature humanity.

I am sure it would be false to equate spiritual growth with any specific degree of human development, but the fact remains that we are called to grow to the fullest of our potential. Human and spiritual growth are intricately inter-twined and go hand in hand.

The paradox of the gospel message is that we must die to self to become truly self. We become self, not by selfishness, but by being selfless. Denying ourselves for others produces growth of self.

Our society has placed much emphasis on self-development, but not enough on the Christian paradox of service for others as the indispensable means and motive for self-growth.

Self-growth, too, is not quantitative. It differs from person to person. It depends on natural talents, circumstances of life, and so many other uncontrollable factors. A rose is not a bird of paradise. Each one of us is different.

This concept is important for us if we wish to have an evangelical attitude toward the handicapped. They mirror fully God's image and have a right to that fullness of growth of which they are capable.

They grow by love and being loved, by accepting and being accepted, by seeking to serve according to their capacities and not just by being served.

One of the most beautiful aspects of the American Church today is this desire to integrate the handicapped into our community in such a way that we can all profit from their presence.

First of all, we must help parents to realize that handicaps in children are not the results of wrong on their part. There is no need for guilt or shame, just acceptance of the mystery of human existence and of God's love.

Secondly, we must be conscious that it is the duty of all of us to help the handicapped lead full human-spiritual lives. Little things count: for example, seeing that our churches have access for those in wheelchairs.

Thirdly, we must be open, not just to the needs of the handicapped, but to learning from them. That dependency that almost necessarily follows from a handicap can be humiliating for them. But so many times we suffer within us greater handicaps that are less visible, not external, and we are too proud to seek help.

Perhaps more than any other contribution, the handicapped force us so often to see life in a less complicated way. Seeing them we can forget our tendency to build up invisible problems to elicit sympathy from others.

Slowly we are realizing that the handicapped are God's chosen creatures on this earth. Do not forget: there will be no handicapped in heaven.

*   *   *

The Christian faith is full of paradoxes. Christ himself mentioned this aspect of his teaching so often: one must die to oneself to live; one must give up one's life to possess life. These paradoxes are but different expressions of the same basic truth: one must participate in Christ's death to share in his resurrection. The folly of the cross must become a practical reality in the life of each Christian in order to enter new life—to rise with Christ.

God became a human being like us that we might share his life. The Christian paradox derives from this historical reality and its consequences. God comes close to us that we might come close to him—but he remains forever transcendent and mysterious. He is the loving Father, revealed to us in and through Christ—the suffering Christ on the cross—and is forever with us in the person of his Spirit.

When we stumble in our prayer, it is the Spirit that prays in us. When we are aware only of our human frailty, it is the suffering Son who is our model. When we find ourselves alone and abandoned, it is the loving Father of the prodigal son who is near us and caring for us. Yet God is always God: he refuses to be capsulized, reduced to our categories, exhausted by our human ways.

When I was a boy and read the lives of the saints, I was always surprised that they could say that they were the least of men, that they considered themselves the greatest of sinners. "Surely," I used to say to myself, "these saints knew they were not committing grave, serious sins. Surely, they could see that there were so many other people around them worse than they. Was all this pious rhetoric?" I think not. The closer one draws to God, the more insignificant, the more imperfect one seems. The contrast becomes greater, not less.

The saints were able to make such comparisons with honesty because they saw themselves in contrast with God, not as compared to their fellow human beings. The emptier and more fragile and more sinful they felt, the more they saw God's fullness. Or perhaps one should say: the more they saw God's fullness, the more fragile they saw themselves. The closer they came to God, the more distant he seemed and the more unfathomable. The more insecure of themselves they felt, the more they sensed the need for his life and support. The nearer they came to despairing of their own power, the more profound their trust in him became. The paradox of sanctity is that the holier one becomes, the less self-reliant one grows and the more conscious of human weakness and frailty; but, simultaneously, the more confident and hopeful one becomes in God and his power. No, the saints were not hypocrites, but God-centered people.

One of the characteristics of true liturgy is that it should make us aware of that transcendent presence of God that surpasses all understanding and at the same time it should help us approach that loving Father who is ever near. True liturgy helps us see who God is and who we are without confusion. The paradox of distance and closeness, emptiness and fullness, sin and life, weakness and trust is not wiped out, but the cross always triumphs in resurrection and God remains God. True liturgy lets God be God, but always approachable and concerned.

The psalmist of old knew these perennial truths, and all we are saying is but a meditation on Psalm 63.

"O God, you are my God whom I seek; for you my flesh pines and my soul thirsts, like the earth, parched, lifeless and without water." It is with this sense of emptiness, of need, of inadequacy that one approaches the altar.

"Thus have I gazed toward you in the sanctuary to see your power and glory. For your kindness is a greater good than life: my lips shall glorify you." If we have candles and incense and vestments, it is not to be exotic, but to point out the presence of that other that surpasses the human situation and to acknowledge his power and his glory. We are reminded of his presence and his kindness and we are moved to glorify him.

"Thus will I bless you while I live: lifting up my hands, I will call upon your name. As with the riches of a banquet shall my soul be satisfied, and with exultant lips my mouth shall praise you." The psalmist did not know of the Eucharist, but he knew the sentiments of one who approaches the eucharistic banquet and sings the praises of a God who so fills man with new life—with his own life. If the psalmist's lips were "exultant" with praise, what adjective should describe our own?

"I will remember you upon my couch, and through the night-watches I will meditate on you: that you are my help, and in the shadow of your wings I shout for joy." Some ask what relationship there is between liturgy and private prayer. The psalmist answers that question for us: that presence of God is not restricted to the sanctuary but stays with him day and night. He takes time to recall it, to reflect on it, to meditate. He senses himself close to God, like a small bird protected by the wings of a vigilant parent and he is full of joy.

Liturgy becomes life. Although exhausted, parched, weary, empty, the psalmist says to God with faith and trust (let us say it with him): "My soul clings fast to you; your right hand upholds me. O God, you are my God whom I seek."

God's Word Challenges Me

How to read a newspaper

The market is flooded today with "How-to" books. I will not add another book, but just a few comments on how to read a daily newspaper in a Christian way.

My thoughts on this subject were provoked by many people who have mentioned to me how disturbed they get when they read the newspapers. It seems to them that the scene painted by the press is one of unrest, violence, and selfishness the world over.

It is not, of course, always the press' fault. They must inform us of what is happening, and disasters do make good matter for ink. One must also be fair and acknowledge the presence of many heartwarming stories of heroism and courage that the papers print.

The dilemma is a real one: we must keep abreast of what is happening in the world and in our city; we must be well-informed and not hide all of this, nor ignore it. Yet I sympathize with the elderly lady who told me recently that she gets very agitated if she watches the evening news on TV or reads the newspapers at night. She has a hard time falling asleep.

I confess that I go through the daily papers pretty fast; but

I began to check my own emotional responses and to ask myself the question—do I sense some of these same sentiments of anxiety and worry and revulsion as I read this?

I was forced to say "yes." Then I began to reflect on how I should react as a Christian to all these accounts of world and local events. The answer? I found myself praying.

So, as I read each disturbing item, I decided to turn my emotional response into a little prayer. I decided not to wait till the General Intercessions at Mass next morning, but to say immediately an earnest prayer.

That prayer did two things for me. It made the text become much more real and alive to me, since I seemed involved. I prayed for real people in the middle of real tragedy. I found myself, with a tear, saying a fervent prayer for a thirteen-year-old prostitute; I said a prayer for a twenty-four year old faced with a drug problem; I prayed for light and wisdom to understand the values at play in Africa.

I prayed also in gratitude for beautiful weather, and with joy for a few comic strips.

Sometimes I just placed everything in the hands of the Lord (the Middle East); sometimes I resolved to get more involved (Fair Housing).

Did I feel I was playing games? No. It suddenly came to me that I was bringing God into a moment in my day where I had never thought of him. Of course, it takes longer to read a paper this way, but time spent on prayer is a bonus, not time wasted.

So, the content of my book—if I were to write one—on how to read a newspaper as a Christian would be very short: Prayerfully.

Hospitality

More recently we have begun to see the need of being more hospitable in our churches. By this I mean that we have to welcome strangers and guests to our liturgical assemblies so that they truly feel wanted. This means that we must reexamine that very Christian virtue of receiving guests and strangers truly as if they were Christ.

A concept of Christian hospitality will also be a force to open us up to not just new people but also to the talents and ideas that they bring with them. But hospitality goes much deeper than that. It must pervade not just our liturgical assemblies but our whole lifestyle.

Many times in Africa I witnessed how families and religious communities went without eating because guests had arrived unexpectedly. Often, too, I saw them make great sacrifices so that no guest would be turned away for the night. They truly treat guests in their culture with dignity and concern. For this same reason I often felt safer as a guest among "pagans" in Africa than among Christians in the U.S.A.

For us, however, hospitality must flow from our conviction of the gospel values: we must follow the Lord's admonition to see himself in the guest, the sick, the poor, the thirsty and the captive.

In our Benedictine monasteries of old, each guest found there a true sanctuary. St. Benedict also warned his monks to receive poor and rich alike, since the image of Christ did not depend on costly robes and jewelry.

Why is hospitality so important as an evangelical witness? Perhaps the first reason is that it should be totally gratuitous, that is, one should not be expecting anything in return. In receiving those categories that Jesus mentioned in the gospel, we find a real test for our own unselfish service. The poor, especially, must be received well, precisely because they cannot pay back in kind: they are stripped and deprived of human goods—just as Jesus was.

Guests, too, are defenseless, that is, they really are at the mercy and will of the host. Perhaps in our own society today this aspect seems less evident, but it will always be partially true. Receiving a guest as if he or she were Jesus means respecting that defenselessness and never taking advantage of it.

On the other side of the coin, we must imitate Jesus as well and be glad to be a guest. He entered the home of Zacchaeus of Matthew, the tax collector, in order to dine there. He accepted the invitation of Martha and Mary and Lazarus for the dinner they had prepared for him. He accepted all the attentions that Simon wished to bestow on him as guest.

In a very strange way, being guest means also losing a bit of one's independence, and in the first cases cited in the life of Jesus we saw that he lost his good name as well!

When one is a guest of another, one can experience that kind of trust that is necessary as well as the bonds of friendship which are implied. The sharing that comes from hospitality, if done in the name of Jesus, will be the basis for a deeper communication.

St. Benedict had good reason then to encourage his monks to be hospitable. But he went even further and reminded them of the special insights that a guest can bring to a family and community. A guest can be more objective and often bring a wider experience. For this reason one must listen most carefully to them, in order to get out of one's own narrowness and complacency.

Especially in our liturgical assemblies, we must be conscious of this kind of hospitality and of creating that warm atmosphere where anyone will feel at home.

Jokingly today, some talk of the "ministry of hospitality" as another term for the ushers. Although this sounds exaggerated, nevertheless it is important that those upon whom this act of receiving guests falls be conscious of their duties to receive all warmly. Whether the ushers be men or women, they must take this task as a part of the groundwork necessary for a good liturgical celebration.

As we pray so often that Jesus will receive us into our final resting home and there participate at our heavenly banquet, let us remember also that he invites us regularly to attend the eucharistic banquet, and in that invitation we have a chance to be constantly his guests. He receives us with open arms. As he has given of himself, so he expects us to give toward others.

Spiritual vertebrates

Have you ever wondered about the phrase in Luke's gospel that Christ grew in wisdom and in age (Lk. 2:52)? If we consider not just the young Jesus, but the life of his Mother and those around him, we see that they, too, grew in understanding and holiness. Mary did not understand fully the message of the angel; she could not have understood the divine plan that would lead her Son to death on the cross; Simeon had said that sorrows would pierce her heart. Although she did not understand all of this, she pondered these words in her heart and grew gradually to understand their mystery.

We are all much impressed by reading in the gospels the account of the calling of the apostles. They followed Christ immediately, abandoning their fishing boats and their homes; but they did not fully understand Christ and his message until after they had received the Spirit at Pentecost. They, too, had to grow in the understanding of their faith in him.

For us this all has an important meaning. Although by our baptism we have been inserted into a new life, we must grow in holiness and understanding. There is no such thing as a static Christian.

But, how do we grow? We must be open to the Spirit, the source of all growth. Perhaps it would be better to say that the life of the Spirit grows in us; we grow in and through the Spirit. "Being open" means, first of all, placing no obstacles to that growth. Sin—the result of our own selfishness—is the first obstacle. Fear—the lack of confidence in God's providence—is the second. "Being open" means also listening, reflecting, praying.

There is no doubt that one grows by opening oneself to outside stimuli; challenges that come to us from life and its events are indeed moments of growth. New ideas, new experiences, new people do challenge us to greater growth and can be valid instruments of the Spirit. But for true growth let us not neglect the sacraments, the reading of the Bible in a prayerful attitude, the liturgical cycle, and all those acts of unselfish love that help us bring Christ to others.

Perhaps part of our fear comes from the fact that we know we cannot absorb everything. We cannot espouse everything. In such a case there would be no continuity, no real growth, but just superficial change, inconstancy, and fickleness. We would become inanimate, porous sponges, full of extraneous material that never becomes a part of us.

But we must also be convinced that we cannot become like those crustaceans, clams and oysters, that live within a shell that admits of no growth. If they open that hard, restricting covering, they will become the prey of every fish in the ocean. No growth is possible, although life may seem to be protected.

The solution? We must all be vertebrates, that is, we must have a backbone. This means that we have strong faith commitments that support us and give to our life continuity and strength. A backbone permits growth: it grows as we grow. The source of our growth is the source of our constancy. It permits us to stand up and face the world. Faith, hope, and love belong to vertebrates. They permit growth, but remain solid.

When Christ spoke of the servant who hid the talents he was given, he warned us against lack of growth, against just preserving our gifts without development. If, by natural instinct, we fear change and new ideas, then we must have more faith in the guiding hand of God in his church and in our lives. If, by natural instinct, we are prone to seek our escape from growth by constant vacillation and in every new fad that comes along, then we must discipline ourselves and spend more time in prayer, reflections, and discernment: we must face up to life with confidence in God and not seek evasions.

What I am saying is that God created us vertebrates and he expects us to grow in sanctity as we face each new moment of existence with the joys and sorrows it brings. Have confidence. He is with us.

Unselfishness

We all yearn to live in a perfect society where there will be peace and understanding among men. Being realistic, we know that it will never come about totally; but still we sense that we must have high ideals and continue to seek to build such a society.

As a model, the first Christian community at Jerusalem stays before our eyes. Every generation of Christians has looked back on the description of that first group with nostalgia. In the Acts of the Apostles (Chap. 2:42-47 and Chap. 4:32-35) we find the following characteristics of that community. "The whole group of believers were united, heart and soul." Such a complete unity, we learn, was based on the fact that they remained "faithful to the teaching of the apostles, to the brotherhood, to the breaking of bread, and to the prayers." Every day they went to the temple to pray but met in their houses for the breaking of bread. Prayer, Eucharist, and faithfulness to the Gospel message were the sources of their profound oneness of heart and mind.

It is good for us to see at once that there is no unity unless Christ himself be its source and foundation. Oneness in faith in his teaching, oneness in his life given us in the Eucharist, oneness in praising him in our prayers—such is the basis of Christian unity.

But the description goes on to tell us about the results of such a spiritual unity: "No one claimed for his own use anything that he had, as everything they owned was held in common." "None of their members was ever in want." "They sold their goods and possessions and shared out the proceeds among themselves according to what each one needed." The church was never again to realize such a complete sharing of goods. But why should the dream disappear? Almost all rules for religious life have drawn on this example of the community of Jerusalem as an inspiration. One of the aims of religious life was to keep alive that example in the church. Although our times might not permit a sharing of all goods in common by all the faithful, simply because of the magnitude of the enterprise, still the ideal of sharing so that no one is in need remains. Moreover, the description tells us that they shared their food "gladly and generously." There was no stinting, no holding back, no sadness in giving up, no accumulating.

It is also told to us that because of this example of unity and charity their numbers grew rapidly and God performed many miracles through them.

But what is it that prevents us from realizing this description in our day? It can be summarized in one word: selfishness. Already St. Paul had to deal with the difficulty at the community of Philippi. Paul pleads with the faithful there to be united in their convictions and love with a common purpose and a common mind. He continues: "There must be no competition among you, no conceit; but everyone is to be self-effacing. Always consider the other person to be better than yourself, so that no one thinks of his own interests first but everybody thinks of other people's interests instead" (Phil. 2:3-4).

Paul then continues with one of the most beautiful and inspiring passages in the whole of the Scriptures. (If I were stranded on a lonely island and could have one chapter of Scripture with me, it would be this second chapter to the Philippians.) To counteract selfishness Paul tells them: "In your minds you must be the same as Christ Jesus: His state was divine, yet he did not cling to his equality with God but emptied himself to assume the condition of a slave, and became as men are; and being as all men are, he was humbler yet, even to accepting death, death on a cross" (Phil. 2:5-8).

Paul sets before us the example of Jesus who emptied himself of his own glory to become like us, to take on the condition of a servant or slave. The Greek word used by theologians of all times to describe the process whereby Christ "emptied himself" is kenosis. He did not seek his own glory, but to serve. It is this example that St. Paul sets before our eyes to be imitated if we wish to live in peace and harmony.

Today in the church everyone is talking of new ministries; but there is no true ministry in the church, whether it be that of pope, bishop, priest, or deacon, unless it be accompanied by the interior disposition that Christ had. All the other services that are also in a broader sense called ministry must derive from this same attitude.

But the Christian paradox continues: precisely because of that obedience to serve even to death on the part of Jesus, he was raised to the right hand of the Father, where every tongue should acclaim him as Lord, to the glory of God the Father. By our own willingness to serve others, to think of their needs and not our own, we come eventually to participate in that same glory. By emptying ourselves of our own ambitions and self-glory, we merit to share in his.

As Paul gave this program to the Church of Philippi that they might live in peace and harmony and be united in conviction and love with a common purpose and a common mind, so I repeat it to all the faithful. "That is the one thing which would make me completely happy" (Phil. 2:2).

Hope and the Eucharist

During the depression years in the thirties, it seemed the end of the world couldn't be far off. There were no signs of hope—just daily struggles to keep alive.

Then came World War II and Korea and Vietnam. The world would continue—but there was no respite from the threat of total destruction.

Today, too, so many live their day-to-day existences in anxiety and fear, without willingly focusing their eyes on the future. Why are there so many teen-age suicides, we ask?

The media, also, seem to dwell on the more depressing aspects of our civilization and the precarious bases its systems are built on. Newspapers sell because people seem to want to read all the gory details of human violence against other humans.

Because a doctor sees only sick patients, he could easily deduce that only sickness exists in the world. Healthy people have no need of doctors.

But if life is erroneously looked at as a constant process of deterioration, then the inevitable result will be depression and anxiety and fear.

The solution, of course, is not to fall into the opposite trap, that is, to pretend that all is always well. There is evil, there is sickness, there is pain, there is disappointment. And, yes, some do seem to get a larger share than others.

For a Christian, however, life can be seen as a purification process from death to resurrection. Suffering is not denied, but given meaning. When Jesus said he was the resurrection and the life, he meant it. He also meant what he said when he told his disciples that those who lived in him would never die.

In Chapter 6 of John's gospel, this astonishing explanation is given to us: Jesus came to give us life and to begin that redemptive, resurrectional process in us that reaches fulfillment only in him. The new food he gives us is a pledge of eternal life.

The context of Chapter 6 of John reflects the effects of the gifts of the Eucharist. The Eucharist always contains that dimension of hope in a blessed future built into it. It is a pledge, as St. Thomas reminds us, of what is to come. But it is not a rain check kind of pledge. It begins what later will reach completion when we obtain the fullness of divine presence and life.

For this reason Eucharist can never be for us Catholics just a sign of fellowship, however deep the bonds of affection that bind us may be.

Eucharist brings us together in unity and fellowship only because we partake of one body of Jesus. *He* is the source of all life, all unity, all love, all fellowship, and all hope.

But Eucharist is still a shadow of what is yet to come. How then could we be anything but hope-filled people?

Mary, May, and Model

Mary, May, and Model

In our moments of joy or sorrow, of courage or hesitation, of strength or weakness, we all need models and examples. It is people who influence and sustain and nurture people. More than anything else, we need the assurance in moments of our own dejection that others have made it. We need models that inspire and animate, that provide positive motivation and that give courage. So many professional people can point out others in the same field—often older and wiser—who were an inspiration to them at the beginning of their careers. How indebted I am to so many old priests and brothers of my community for the example of their strong Faith, for their deep awareness of God's presence in their lives, for their confidence in his providence!

Catholic tradition has given special attention to narrating the heroic lives of the saints for this very reason. We are all called upon to imitate Jesus, the supreme model. One could perhaps think, thus, that his example and the gospels alone would be enough. But we humans often need more. Seeing how others have fulfilled this mandate of imitating him is both inspiring and helpful.

One should not forget, too, the fruits of competition.

84

Winning for its own sake is not important—certainly not winning against others; but competition, with all its mutual incentives and urging for greater achievement, is natural to all. St. Paul knew this and saw his own life in terms of a competitive race. He, too, was not afraid to tell the Christian communities he had formed to imitate him. All basketball or football coaches—or people involved in any sport—know the value of the competitive spirit. One runs faster if the competition is stiffer and if the whole group is alive and excited.

The asceticism of the early church was geared toward martyrdom. All life was seen as a preparation for that kind of possible death: it was a contest, an *agonia*. The example of the faith, the endurance, the courage, and the ability to forgive that is found in the stories of the early martyrs was to inspire all of us to a greater sanctity. How much of that desire for holiness we have lost!

But among all models Mary stands out as the first and the finest. She is for us. Even the revelation of her Immaculate Conception and of her final destiny, her assumption into heaven, is not just to satisfy our intellectual curiosity, but to give us signs of God's love and providence for his creatures, signs of hope and consolation for us all.

The Dogmatic Constitution on the Church of Vatican II (*Lumen Gentium*) put it this way: "In the bodily and spiritual glory which she possesses in heaven, the Mother of Jesus continues in this present world as the image and first flowering of the church as she is to be perfected in the world to come. Likewise, Mary shines forth on earth, until the day the Lord shall come, as a sign of sure hope and solace for the pilgrim people of God" (par. 68).

Perhaps again today we are becoming aware of the need we have in our lives for models of hope and signs of God's loving providence. We live in an age of pessimism, of continuous change and the resultant insecurity. Not only do we have many personal sufferings, but we find ourselves also surrounded by so many situations where we have no control over the conditions that affect us. It is so easy for us to become totally absorbed by the cares of each day, by the worries of making a living, by the pain of suffering in our personal lives and in our relationship to others. We need models of hope, models of those who have suffered too, but who remained faithful to the wishes of the Lord. The glimpse of Mary should be an encouragement. Just as God did marvels for her, so he will do marvels for me.

But Mary goes beyond being just a sign. As she was the Mother of Jesus in the flesh, so her Motherhood continues on in a special way. Just as Mary was united so intimately to Jesus on earth, so she is united to him now as he continues to be the source of our redemption and all our grace. But just as she is united to Jesus, so she is united to his church. Mary's particular role in the life of Jesus gives her also a special place and function in the church. She is often cited as the model of its faith, its charity, and of perfect union with Christ. Just as she gave birth to Jesus, the source of all new life, so the church is seen as giving birth to divine life in each one of us. The church should be that place of special union between ourselves and the divine life of Jesus.

Models must be imitated, not just looked at. The same Vatican II document succinctly spelled out the qualities that Mary had that were needed for her mission: "Believing and obeying, Mary brought forth on earth the Father's Son" (63). Believing and obeying! The source of all the marvels of her life was God responding to her *Fiat*, her "Yes." The fact that she said her "Yes" to the invitation of the Father to be the Mother of his Son is the source of all other marvels that happened to her. It is not enough just to look on Mary as our model of joy and solace, if we are not willing to imitate her in her obedience and in her faith. We must be able to see the marvels of the past that God has done for his people—especially for Mary—and accept with our own *Fiat* the challenge of the present and of the future.

To be like her we must obey, say our "Yes," accept God's

plan and will in moments of obscurity and without assurance. This means we do not seek our selfish ways, but what will contribute to his kingdom.

Obeying means being sensitive to the voices around one—listening. Mary could not have brought forth new life if she had not been open to the Spirit. No one can beget new life alone. We, too, have to be receiving from others—and especially from the Holy Spirit—since only in this way will we be sensitive to God's will, have new life within us, and reach out in an unselfish way to others.

May is Mary's month, since it, too, is the living symbol of freshness and new life.

May is a time to say thanks to God for Mary and for all the new life he has given to us to take courage, as, listening to the Spirit, we say again our *Fiat*.